The Voyage Out

'That was the strange thing, that one did not know where one was going, or what one wanted, and followed blindly, suffering so much in secret, always unprepared and amazed and knowing nothing; but one thing led to another and by degrees something had formed itself out of nothing, and so one reached at last this calm, this quiet, this certainty, and it was this process that people called living.'

Virginia Woolf, *The Voyage Out*

The Voyage Out: An Anthology

Edited by Kirsty Gunn and Gail Low

The Voyage Out Press

First published in Great Britain in 2016 by The Voyage Out Press
Copyright © of texts and images remains with the authors 2016
Cover design and art work © Sian MacFarlane 2016
Typeset by Sian MacFarlane

Printed by Winter and Simpson Print
16 Dunsinane Avenue
Dunsinane Industrial Estate
Dundee DD2 3QT

ISBN 978-0-9955123-0-6

The publisher gratefully acknowledges the support of the
University of Dundee and Dundee Heritage Trust.

The Voyage out Press

Contents

Contents

Contents

For Jim Stewart

1952 - 2016

Kirsty Gunn & Gail Low

Notes towards a journey

'Words, words, words… They're all we have to go on…' So says some character in some play, alluding to some other play about a certain somewhat wordy Danish Prince…

All words – words, and more words – and yet just look what happens when we take the words away. Though we may know how to fill in the gaps in this instance – the play is Tom Stoppard's Rosencrantz and Guildenstern are Dead, that super -literary talk-talk-talk drama about the gaps in between the scenes of Hamlet – nevertheless isn't it interesting when we let this information slide off the sentence? When we let go of the certainties of facts, of naming, definitive language, and can't go forwards… It's as though we come to feel ourselves to be imprecise – careless, even if the slippage is deliberate. For we do become different people when we talk in a different way. Especially us, the sort of people in this lecture theatre, the sort of people who are interested in listening to and describing things, who may read and write for a living – how changed we are, how we barely recognise ourselves when we become the people who don't name, don't define but instead just let meaning, like teenagers, hang.

For that's where language can take us, for sure. To a wild and lonely place that can make us curious and weird and anti-social and a little mad. Pushed into a different kind of creativity that, rather than reflect our imagination, actually informs it, creates it. Because why, with such literary precedents, when the whole history of English Literature, after all, is to do with shaking up and reforming sentences, should the idea persist that we need to be so certain with our words? Or at least, why need we be so certain so much of the time?

We may not get on without clarity and probity and definition but there most surely is a place in our creative, 'making' lives for vagueness, disquietude, craziness even. What if we close our eyes and, to paraphrase William Carlos Williams, wait to know what we mean by seeing what we say.

(Kirsty Gunn, 'Letting Words Go', 2006)

When Kirsty Gunn all but skipped up to the front of the hall to deliver her inaugural professorial lecture, 'Letting Words Go', there seemed to be an disjuncture between the slip of a girl as she seemed to me then, and the academic position she was to inhabit. Here was a most unprofessorial persona who used words and phrases such as 'craziness', letting 'meaning, like teenagers, hang' in institutional spaces of learning – not to mention her use of 'groovy' or 'funky' in earlier conversations. What kind of professor spoke like that? That disquiet expanded into full blown incredulousness when she declared, 'I want to say that it's the letting go, of definitives in our language, of the limited ways we describe ourselves, that opens us up to possibilities. To ask ourselves instead: what happens next? And what will I learn by allowing myself not to know?' Despite her fame, friendliness and her string of novels what did she know about *teaching* writing? Could creative writing be taught?

As a scholar in literary studies, there was something puzzling counterintuitive (scandalous even) in that assertion, said with airborne certainty and conviction, that we could write without compass coordinates for the routes we take, that we would not always need to plot a course to control points like some relentless orienteer. That our writing needn't be some ocean-going vessel existing simply to disgorge cargo at the journey's end.

There is, of course, nothing wrong with writing that needs to convey information, a largesse of knowledge to unload – where would the world be without cargo ships? But the challenge remains of allowing permeability between different modes, of not always having to police borders. Writing should not always have to be linear, rigidly goal-oriented. 'Dreaming with my eyes open' was one of those phrases that ambushed me, but which I had dismissed as romantic, sentimental rhetoric.

Ten years down the line, returning to that lecture now, I am astonished at how much of it proved prescient of my own learning how to write again. It is not as if I have abandoned scholarly writing (I haven't), but I have learnt to see words as things in themselves. To see that words have quiddity, weight and music, that intention and meaning are not transparently conveyed. That language can be chimerical, devious with a life of its own. Keeping an expressive openness to the different kinds of writing is damned tricky, sometimes leading to an abyss and, more often than not, resulting in heated arguments and red pencil edits. Yet I see that this is the only way to go.

Kirsty Gunn & Gail Low

Notes towards a journey

"a willingness to take risks, to take up the challenge to see the world outside disciplinary tramlines, to inhabit spaces betwixt and between all too familiar modes of seeing"

Voyages of these kind – beginnings without the necessary certainties of charted routes – are unsettling but they are also worth the while. 'What if… we wait to know what we mean by seeing what we say', she had said.

This volume speaks to all of the qualities that leaven Writing Practice and Study at Dundee: a willingness to take risks, to take up the challenge to see the world outside disciplinary tramlines, to inhabit spaces betwixt and between all too familiar modes of seeing; to think about that vibrant matter of language, its assemblages as much as its function to express and inform – the brightness of being amidst the necessary steel and glass of the knowledge industry. We asked our contributors to imagine a thought experiment, 'What if…' What if you linked the personal and the scholarly as complementary modes? What if you inflected the essay or the short story with a lyric voice, colliding two different modes? What if you imagined the relevance and impact your research has on the ways you actually think and live? What if you let us know something of the fear, angst and also the sheer joy of starting out on a journey: the mystery of beginnings, the enigma of arrivals.

(Gail Low, 'Beginning Again', 2016)

'An adventure, of sorts, this is' we had both said to all those who are part of *The Voyage Out*. We thought about RRS *Discovery*, that glorious rigged and sea-ready vessel with its high mast and narrow quarters that took Scott and Shackleton to Antarctica and is moored here at Dundee, looking for all the world as though it would take only a high wind and a breath of imagination for it to snap its rigging, and set off down the Tay again towards the wide open seas. 'That kind of adventure', we said to the writers, artists, scientists, historians, publishers and poets all gathered here, within our own kind of ship, quartered in these lovely pages. 'Imagine what you might contribute as being your own kind of voyage' we said. 'Just as your work is an experiment and a question and a grand game... Think about going out onto the great white expanse as the *Discovery* went out there. Into nothingness, into the unknown...' And one by one, the contributors in the pages that follow stepped on board.

For each one, exploring those wide uncharted waters meant something different; for each, the response to that question had about it a degree of the unexpected. What a thrill it was for us to receive back work that struck out with an idea of risk about it, of, in some cases, uncertainty even.

As teachers of writing here at Dundee, our imagination is only widened by holding that same kind of 'what-if' about every project. Asking ourselves, our students, to imagine the bounds of the written word as something that exists much further away from home or comfort zones; asking literary criticism to take account of literariness, less an imposition of meaning and more a willingness to converse with texts; asking that the writing of stories, plays and poems takes a leap of imagination rather than conforming to the standard, and pushing always, the idiosyncratic over the acceptable, the unknown over the familiar.

'Writing Practice and Study' we call our discipline here at Dundee – so to practise, over and over, the lonely, crazy business of sitting alone with an empty sheet of paper before us, to fill up that white sheet with its world of words. And then to study, and study again, yes, one's own work, but more, the work of others: reading so as to write, to be disciplined in our risk taking, self-aware and formal in our wild 'otherness'... This, too, is how *The Voyage Out* celebrates, marks achievement and bravery. We mourn the passing of our friend and colleague, Jim Stewart – poet, scholar, critic and teacher. Yet, in the totality of these pages, we also celebrate his curiosity about these different spheres reflected here, and his ability to both marvel at and hold them all within his ken. So what you'll make of what is ahead – as with any voyage – is over to you. Now that you're on board, welcome, we say. Let's see what happens here.

(Kirsty Gunn & Gail Low, 'Notes towards a journey', *The Voyage Out*, July 2016)

Jim Stewart

Vessel

light O boat ticking over the deep,
a twitch on that broadest of backs,
no mark visible from the miles above
or miles under the abyss – midge,
straw-fleck adrift in its wide sky,
why do you do what you do and point
your minor ingenuity
and small magnificence
at an overwhelming light
too great for you to look at,
which will quietly absorb you
if and when you arrive?

wrath anger is reasonable and righteous,
but cross the line and something more than this
awaits, or worse, comes seeking.
It will not bargain or listen to a plea
made too late; will take the shape
of a northern threat, its rigging of bolts
the nerves of light in the first spit
of an inconceivable downpour.
Sail on, storm-blind. As you wish.
Keep your course, rebellious heart.
It will not save you.

mercy finally, after great foolishness,
the advent of calm
that follows the idiot risks
and the long-unanswered prayer,
with only these little splashes to the side
to indicate motion. Stillness on the deep,
move, boat. It hardly matters where.
Darkness full upon the broken waters,
let creation begin.

History

Christopher A Whatley

Auld acquaintance: Robert Burns at home
and away in the nineteenth century

"He never left Scotland.
But his work did."

Robert Burns nowadays is Scotland's global super-
star. In a poll organized by the National Trust
for Scotland in the spring of 2016, he was voted
the greatest Scot – and not for the first time.
Tens of thousands of suppers and similar events
celebrating his birthday are held annually on 25th
January on most of the world's continents. His
works can be read in more than forty languages,
including, most recently, Chinese.

Yet Burns was first and foremost a local poet.
Indeed he described himself as Coila's rustic bard,
Coila being the muse of that part of Ayrshire –
Kyle - in which he had been raised and where he
wrote his early poetry and from which he drew
much of his imagery and inspiration. Most of the
subscribers to the first edition of his *Poems* were
inhabitants of the small inland town of Kilmarnock and its vicinity, where the volume was published in 1786.[1] He had been born in a relatively
humble cottage in the rural hamlet of Alloway,
near to the coastal burgh of Ayr, and thirty-seven
years later died in the county town of Dumfries,
only sixty miles distant. He never left Scotland.
but his work did. Even before his early death in
July 1796 Burns's poetry had crossed the Irish
Sea to Ulster, where he was much esteemed by
Ulster's weaver poets, perhaps for the radicalism
of his sentiments and certainly for his use of the
Scots language – which was similar to their own.[2]
By the early 1790s the Kilmarnock edition, as
well as that published in Edinburgh the following
year had survived the transatlantic crossing to
reach the North American towns of New York
and Philadelphia.[3] By the 1800s Burns was
being read by Scots in India – his countrymen

Christopher A Whatley

Auld acquaintance: Robert Burns at home and away
in the nineteenth century

"And what is interesting – are
the ways in which Burns was
read on or, more precisely, at
the end of these voyages out."

drawn there in their droves by the opportunities
created by service in the East India Company
but conscious too that the risks entailed in the
sea journey there and back, the unfamiliarly hot
climate, and disease, made the search for eastern
riches a high-priced lottery.

And what is interesting – and the focus of this
essay – are the ways in which Burns was read on
or, more precisely, at the end of these voyages out.

Burns spoke with many voices. As a poet he was
an enigma, as he was as a man. Well over two
centuries after his death there is still uncertainty
about his politics. Was he a revolutionary or a
radical? Or a constitutional Whig who on occasion
even spoke out for the Tories? A Scottish patriot
or a Scottish nationalist or, latterly, a loyal Briton?[4]
Even prior to his death in 1796 his legacy was con-
tested, and afterwards plundered in the interests of
competing visions of Scottish society. Up until the
middle of the nineteenth century the main pulls
were between Scotland's conservatives and the
country's Radicals – including the Chartists. The
former – mainly Tories and aristocrat led – were
concerned about the threat to the prevailing social
order posed by revolutions abroad, and utilized as
a bulwark against change. This, they argued,
portrayed rural Scotland at its best: patriarchal,
stoical, God-fearing, and stable. Radicals on the
other hand drew on Burns's songs, above all 'Is
there, for honest poverty' ('A Man's a Man'), with
its declaration of the worth of all human beings
regardless of rank or wealth, sentiments that
lifted spirits and inspired working class struggles
in both the workplace and political spheres.

Indeed as an agent of change – as a figure who had some influence in shaping Scottish history in the nineteenth century in particular – most historians have overlooked Burns.[5] His role in sustaining the idea of Scotland, and national pride within the England-dominated United Kingdom, was also critical. It would be surprising if it had been otherwise: across Europe during what was a time of growing awareness of national history and consciousness, from Jacint Verdaguer in Catalonia to Alexander Pushkin in Russia, patriotic poets were in the vanguard.

Overseas, Burns was also read intensely, although drawn upon to support particular causes, and given different emphases. This is not to say that Burns's radicalism had no impact once his poems and songs left Scottish shores. On the contrary. We have noted already the admiration there was for him – as a 'ploughman poet' – and his work in Ulster. In North America there are strong indications that Burns was one of several poets and writers whose themes and use of satire influenced the future United States President, Abraham Lincoln. So too, it appears, did the pulsating cadences of Burns's poems, which Lincoln drew on in his oratory.[6] In India links have been established between readings of Burns by Bengali students in the 1820s and their recitation of the lines 'man to man the world o'er/Shall brothers be and a' that' against the Hindu caste system; his work provided sustenance for the seeds of Indian nationalism.[7] He was avidly read too in many European countries, and, by the later nineteenth century and above all in the twentieth century, he had become an iconic figure for democratic and socialist movements; and,

ultimately, for socialist and communist states.[8] Yet, as striking – certainly for Scots abroad – is the way Burns induced a heightened sense of nostalgia and a longing for home. In fact this is how Burns was promoted by his first editors, with James Currie for instance hoping that the edition of Burns's poems he had sent to a Royal Navy captain friend would 'charm you with the strains of nature, and awake in your memory the scenes of your early days.'[9] Writing in 1846, Lieutenant Colonel George Veitch, back in Scotland after serving in India, reflected how the 'name of Burns had ever operated like a charm amid the regrets of banishment', and how in his poetry and song 'we used to triumph over the sorrows of exile.'[10] Burns soon became the epitome of what from the moment of departure was Scotland remembered, and over time imagined.[11]

Burns's sentimental work had no shortage of admirers in Scotland. Indeed there are those who have argued that this was his primary appeal: the poet of a rural order that was rapidly disappearing, trampled underfoot by the march of agrarian capitalism in the name of improvement.[12] That this assessment ignores Burns's importance as the 'people's poet', who had articulated their grievances and on their behalf won respect from the classes who had formerly expected unquestioning deference need not detail us here. What matters is the evidence – documentary and visual – that sustains the proposition that overseas Burns was often commemorated, celebrated and employed in ways that could differ from what happened in Scotland. It was *furth* (or outside) of Scotland that the 'thirst of nostalgia' was most intense.

Christopher A Whatley

Auld acquaintance: Robert Burns at home and away
in the nineteenth century

in the United States Burns's egalitarian ideals had
to a degree already been achieved. That a more
passive role in contemporary politics was accorded
to Burns on the other side of the Atlantic can be
inferred from a letter by the Scots-born steel mag-
nate, philanthropist and Burns devotee Andrew
Carnegie, regretting his nonattendance at the
Albany inauguration in 1888, but pronouncing
it fitting that 'the land of Triumphant Democracy
should produce his [Burns's] best memorial.'[13]
Celebrations of Burns, therefore, may have been
acts of confirmation and perhaps even self-con-
gratulation. In Canada, furthermore, and in sharp
contrast to Scotland, working people on such
occasions were less numerous and appear even to
have been ignored, or deliberately excluded. By
this means Burns was stripped of his democratic
associations and became instead a symbol around
which the respectable citizenry could indulge in a
consensual celebration of their Scottish roots but
without any hint of patriotic or any other kind of
passion that might upset the status quo.[14]

Emblems associated with Scotland were visible
at Scottish unveiling ceremonies, but usually as
part of a mix of symbols, including the British
Union Jack flag. By contrast, what organizers in
North America emphasized was their Scottishness
(although it was an American flag that covered
Central Park's and Albany's Burns statutes prior
to their unveiling, not a Scottish lion rampant or
a British Union Jack).[15] The procession at Central
Park in 1880 prior to the unveiling of the Burns
statue there (by the Scottish sculptor, Sir John
Steell) was formed by members of the Caledonian
clubs of Brooklyn, Hudson, and Newark, 'dressed

Let us take the example of North America – and
what we can learn from the ceremonies accom-
panying the unveiling of the ubiquitous statues
of Burns that were erected there between 1880
and the 1920s. For one thing, on the whole,
crowds were smaller, but also there was less of the
emotional energy and ardor that were palpable
in Scotland. The explanation for this may be that

in the Highland costume.'[16] In Fredericton in October 1906, the pageant comprised two brass bands and a group of pipers, along with members from two clan societies, many dressed in kilts or wearing sashes and sporting sprays of heather. In Chicago, 'kilted warriors' stood out.[17] The emphasis, therefore, was on Highland Scotland, even though Burns was primarily a Lowland poet. But for those so bedecked, this was Scotland of yore (and a Scotland that most of those so garbed had never known), a far-off land that had by then been romanticized further by Sir Walter Scott. Although the main speaker at Fredericton, D. C. Fraser, lieutenant governor of Nova Scotia, concluded his address with a stirring assurance that 'It's coming yet for a' that' (i.e., the brotherhood of man), it was as a prompt for men and women to reminisce about 'the old land' that he envisaged the newly unveiled Burns statue. Amongst Scots overseas, this – Scotland's past – was a familiar trope.[18]

But while many in North America acknowledged Burns's patriotism and the strength of feeling émigré Scots had for their homeland, as was remarked by George William Curtis at the unveiling of the Burns statue in New York's Central Park, Burns's 'imperishable patriotism' should not be limited 'by any nationality or country.' In this sense Burns was not only portable, he was also adapted to meet North American needs. This is confirmed by looking at the dates chosen for unveiling ceremonies. In Scotland, the date chosen for the international centenary celebration of Burns's birth in 1859 was 25 January, his birthday. This was also the date for the unveiling of the first free-standing statue of Burns, in Glasgow, in 1877. Yet for the Albany equivalent in 1888, 30 August was fixed upon despite having no associations with Burns; instead it coincided with the annual gathering of the Caledonian Association. Even more clearly US-centric was Denver, Colorado, where the date for the unveiling was the Fourth of July 1904.[19] Toronto's Burns was unveiled on Thanksgiving Day 1906.

Burns's 'voyage out' in the direction of North America, then, resulted in somewhat different emphases being placed on his legacy than in his home country. In Scotland, amongst other things, Burns was recruited in the cause of social and political change, and played a formative role in the campaigns to maintain a meaningful sense of Scottish nationhood within the British state that had been created with the Union of 1707. But at least until World War One speakers on Burns on both sides of the Atlantic continued to emphasize not only Burns's humanity but also his 'political gospel', the rights and brotherhood of man. Even so, and despite the pitfalls of generalization, it is difficult to avoid the conclusion that in the land of his birth Burns was, in the century after his death, an inspirational poet for the here and now. For many of his fellow Scots (and their descendants) who had voyaged to India and North America, he represented a Scotland that they had left behind but, through his verse and song, could be fondly recalled.

Art

Pat Law

Leaving Pyramiden

Founded in arctic Svalbard in 1927, Pyramiden was once a Russian mining town of 1,000 residents, but abandoned in 1998 at a few days notice – the Russian government no longer able or willing to keep it functioning.

At the time of construction, Pyramiden, named after the hill which rose above the town, was hailed by Russia as being visionary and progressive; the architecture was considered and attention to detail substantial. There was great effort to make the environment as familiar to the residents as the places they had left behind, to the extent that Siberian grass was imported and planted in the main square. Whole families lived here with a school, arts centre, swimming pool, play-park, bars, sports centre, community centre.

Many of the young people may have known nowhere else but this strange and carefully made home - and suddenly they had to leave it. The mixed thoughts and emotions of the residents as they boarded the ship on departure, can only be left to our imaginations.

Vincent O'Sullivan

What's that they say in the theatre,
when you go?

We love the story don't we
of Tennyson, the grand codger, sitting
up in bed, reading his Shakespeare
song, leaning back on sage
Victorian pillows, thinking 'That's enough
for one century,' not
fearing the sun, the heat of the sun, past
winters, this winter's rages, dead
as a hero is dead. On time, for time.

Or Chekhov that loveliest of men
sipping on champagne, imagined it
as a doctor, one supposes, time and time
again, though this time was special,
like ordering oysters in the poshest bar,
this was knowing the serf in the soul
put down once and for all.
Then the train, as so often, to Moscow.
Droll, even for Chekhov.

We envy the poise, the epigrams,
whatever the words that distract,
if not us, then those who crave distraction.
Bravo, our abiding approval, *isn't that
life, all over?* As if rehearsals
paid off once the theatre burns,
the curtain smokes, the gallery offering coins for
goods received. *Perform*,
the last word that rings. The script
by now forgotten. Stagestruck. Speechless.

Vincent O'Sullivan

Takes all sorts, Henri

The trouble is when looking at a Matisse
I'm inclined not to look at the painting
in front of my eyes, so much as the man painting the
picture before it was there to take in,
brilliant as it hangs that instant,
which simply isn't the picture I so attend.

I fancy I know Matisse as I think
of him working, how he fathoms *towards*
rather more than *there*, the marvellous thing
which he knows to be so exactly *is*,
voila, while the fact of it's not yet *done*,
having yet to arrive, is what so commands.

I know aesthetically, Henri, this is perverse.
I know a rotund man with a palette-wide beard
and a wife he loves but can't get on with,
might be at the start or the end or the middle
of as many stories as one likes to imagine,
I know that. Yet it's he enthralls me,

for being so anyone, really, and his working
intently on something so stunning as this turns out,
the genius of arriving just to stand here,
so - but all that clamour *still on its way,*
that's the bit I like thinking, even now. How
perfect he must have thought them, lilacs almost there.

Vincent O'Sullivan

As his wife insists

You must know I'm delighted, Lazarus, having you
home. I *am*. Those lovely things
not easily forgotten – your hand on
my hair, your special laugh for the twins,
'How angels neigh,' as you tease them. As if
you need telling,

now naked again, beside me,
the print from the too tight grave-wraps cut
there still against your skin.
'It'll fade in a day,' – did He tell you
that? Just give me time, she asks him.
Will you do that, love?

Vincent O'Sullivan

Space craft, morning tea

It wasn't 'a matter of significance' of the kind she
liked to announce when advising clients,
but she thought of what she read and was glad
she had read it, 'as if it's likely to matter,'
though it did, she knew that:
                                                     how that famous
message they blasted into outer space,
carrying Bach and the sound of whales, human
greetings, other things the scientists defined
as earthly enticements to spell out *us*,
tell whomsoever receives our golden disc,
'This is earth, arriving': yet no sex,
the advisers decided, no mention of war,
we'll not gift them the secrets that so define us.
Our lies piercing on and on, the next million years.

Poetry

Vincent O'Sullivan

Out of bounds

I've heard of or read three times
in the past fortnight, books with their stories of
stone walls walking in the dead of night,
boulders redefining boundaries under cover of
sleep, a priest saying 'No, I understand,
but No,' to a suicide's mother in her best mauve scarf,
unable to throw earth he craved
on her son so out of bounds –
                            Love being the word
so hard to chisel on the softest stone.
As a man who neither believes nor disbelieves
('the dog's warm vomit' – know the text?)
I'm on the side of the fences wandering through
the night, the jittery moon's compliance,
the shuffle of fellow corpses along the line-
'He took the short cut to get here.

                    Let's let him in.'

Essay

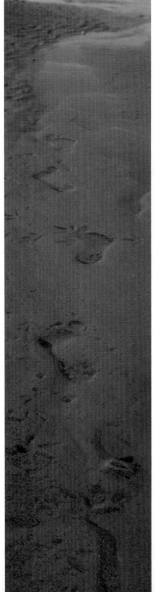

Chris Arthur

Footnotes

My daughter is still young enough not to feel self-conscious about sitting on my knee. I'll miss it when she crosses whatever Rubicon it is that makes children think they're too old to indulge in such physical closeness. When she settles on my lap she's often barefoot. This prompts me to knead her feet, gently pull her toes, stroke her soles firmly enough not to tickle, squeeze the thick skin on her heels. She doesn't mind - I think enjoys – this affectionate caressing of her feet. It's something I've done since she was tiny, when a foot was no longer than my thumb. An evening will often find us thus, sitting contentedly together, her feet warm in my hands.

~

Sitting contentedly together....

That's such a partial truth it courts dishonesty. A measure of contentment is there; it's part of what I feel. But the contentment is fragile. The way in which her bare feet respond and how, in turn, my hands react to the silent prompts delivered by her toes, is almost like a silent language. Its wordless sentences eloquently express affection. But they can also spell out something disconcerting. It's as if, in their soft tattoo of reciprocal movements, the subtly exchanged pressures of touch, our hands and feet sometimes unwittingly semaphore a password, form a secret sign, tap out a combination that opens an unsuspected vault hidden right at the heart of their little intimacies. In it sits something wonderful and terrible. Whenever I glimpse it I sink into a kind of reverie, haunted by disturbing images.

At such moments, her curiosity sparked by my change of mien, my daughter invariably asks me what I'm thinking. I always give the same reply: 'Nothing.'

'Nothing' is, of course, a lie.
I feel increasingly guilty when I tell it.
This is my attempt to tell the truth.

~

'Meditation on a foot' was how I used to think of the state of mind that's sometimes engendered when I hold my daughter's bare feet in my hands. But it isn't a good description. Like 'sitting contentedly' it contains only a trace of truth. 'Meditation' has a philosophical or religious ring. It suggests a mind that's disciplined, untroubled, one that obediently follows well-trodden steps – all safely sanctioned by tradition – in order to reach a point of inner calm and insight. 'Meditation' is something controlled, deliberate and focused. To me, it conjures up the picture of a robed figure, serene, straight-backed and sitting cross-legged, saturated with the kind of composure that betokens unshakeable tranquility. What happens in my mind is altogether less benign, more frantic, sometimes close to panic. The feet I'm holding – so alive in the voltage of vitality they carry – seem able every now and then to kick-start a particular train of thought. Its momentum increases so rapidly that it soon plunges off the rails of easy labeling and becomes a kind of rogue meditation, something that, far from focusing and calming, distracts and disturbs the mind with a dizzying blizzard of impressions.

I imagine the promise of new feet implicit at the moment of conception and how, before dying, they'll become old feet, the skin dry and papery, the nails thickened, the skin threaded with a tracery of broken veins. Then, between these two poles, a flood of images pours through my mind's eye. I picture the microscopic processes of orchestration that shepherd an embryo's undifferentiated cells into the body parts they'll form, conducting the story of their growth and aging. Like reciting a kind of manic rosary, or walking between Stations of the Cross that have proliferated uncontrollably, my imagination runs through a cluster of key moments: the emergence of recognizable foot shapes in the womb; her feet at birth, captivating in the beauty of their miniature twinned perfection; the first time I touched her toes; the first steps she took unaided; the delight that was evident the first time she paddled in the sea; her first steps in a new country; wearing new shoes on her first day at school; solemnly shod in black at the first funeral she went to. My imagination tries to encompass all the steps that have led to this moment, sitting on my knee, her bare feet cupped in my hands. It's as if their soles have engraved upon them a swirling filigree of hidden Braille and that running my fingers over its invisible curlicues I can read the milestones on her walk to here.

~

Sometimes I ask her, 'Where do you think these feet will take you?'

It's an odd way to inquire about what she plans to do with her life. I'm keen to find out where she

Chris Arthur

Footnotes

"Thinking about where her feet will really take her, I reflect on the state of the world and the nature of humanity; the terrible things that we do to one another. I look into the dark corners of my heart and see flickering there traces of the very things I fear may assail her."

wants to go, what she wants to do, where she sees herself in five or ten years from now. I know that wherever her steps may lead, it will be her heart and mind that decides the direction; it's not as if her feet will take her anywhere of their own accord. But when she's sitting on my knee and I'm holding her bare feet in my hands, thinking about all the steps they've taken, all the journeys they'll embark on, it's easy to give them a priority I know they don't really warrant, simply because of the active role they play in bringing her to all her destinations.

She's still young enough not to be much interested in speculating about the future. She's more focused on the immediacies of family, friends, school, food and fashion. But she always answers – or deflects – my question. Her manner is usually patiently dismissive; polite but not entirely serious. She tells me that her feet will take her to China, or Peru, or to somewhere sunny, or to chocolate, or the moon, or 'Away from your silly questions.'

Thinking about where her feet will really take her, I reflect on the state of the world and the nature of humanity; the terrible things that we do to one another. I look into the dark corners of my heart and see flickering there traces of the very things I fear may assail her. However geographically distant they may be, so many of the horrors reported on the news have their roots in nothing more remote or alien than human nature. I know her proximity to peril. And so, although I'm not blind to the beautiful and benign sides of life, and wish them for her in abundance, I worry the same worry that has always troubled parents: the fear that our children's feet will be placed on paths that bring them hurt. I worry that my daughter will tread too trustingly on ground that's treacherous, that she'll walk too close to those who mean her harm.

—

'What are you thinking about, Dad?'
'Nothing.'

In fact I'm thinking about the story of her feet from the moment of their conception until now, the places they've been, the paths they'll follow. I'm thinking of the feet that will walk towards her, be welcomed by her, help kindle within her the tiny feet of whatever offspring she may bear. I'm thinking of the children she may dandle on her knee, perhaps play with their feet and remember the way I used to play with hers. I'm thinking of her feet standing at my graveside and walking away into a future in which I'm absent. I'm thinking about her feet growing old and one day dying. I'm thinking about the power and the powerlessness of love, about how little time we have together.

—

Even focused on no more distant horizons than my daughter's single life, her one individual existence from embryo to corpse, I find my foot-musings disconcerting. But they become much more so when the focus widens to create a perspective in which all of us become like dust specks, or sand grains, or whatever other well-worn metaphor is

chosen to highlight personal insignificance. Instead of starting with her own coming into being, the imagination reaches back through the timeline that led to that moment, picturing the ancestors that stretch back, two by two, far beyond me and my wife, our parents, their parents, until it becomes a blur of predecessors paired in the ghostly umbilical that's stowed within the ark of every person's history. Each ark's manifest records a cargo showing that the individual vessel depends for its existence on those who stand before it – the anchor chain of inheritance stretching back so far in time it's hard to put it into any ready measure. Our mundane calibration of days and months and years is soon exploded by the fact that it's taken eons to shape us. Our bloodline plummets through time's strata; it reaches back to single-celled organisms and their slow ascent to humanness.

Sometimes, my daughter sitting on my knee, I feel crushed by the swarm of lives before and after ours, the crowd of others so dense that it squeezes us to almost nothing. Sometimes I'm awed by the grandeur of the saga that we're part of – our sentient presence, evolved over millennia, walking on this four-and-a-half-billion-year-old planet circling a burning star.

—

'What are you thinking about, Dad?'
'Nothing.'

'Nothing' has some small claim to truth, but I don't mean by it anything as innocuous as the 'nothing much' implied. I'm thinking about how nothing

Chris Arthur

Footnotes

"I'm thinking about how nothing will be left of us, how we'll leave no trace, how such precious moments as these are fated to oblivion."

will be left of us, how we'll leave no trace, how such precious moments as these are fated to oblivion. And this makes me think of my daughter's feet not as anything familiar, not as something set in the unique fixity of this one cherished person, but rather as pieces of life-ore – shaped and moulded countless times before they set into the singular specificity of her body. I'm thinking of the 800,000 year old footprints recently discovered in Happisburgh, Norfolk. And, since the prints of both adults and children were found there, I'm wondering if, among those who left these intimate yet anonymous traces, there might have been a father who held his daughter's feet and wondered where they'd take her.

Africa holds the earliest fossilized footprints yet discovered that display our modern foot's anatomy. They are some 1.5 million years old. Yet more ancient tracks have been found, also in Africa. There's a trail of prints that's 3.7 million years old, left by *Australopithecus afarensis* as these creatures walked across volcanic ash in Laetoli, Tanzania. I think of all the steps we hominids have taken, all the steps that are to come, the individual story each foot tells and the greater story it is part of – for the tread of the species imprints all of us with its mark, as we all contribute our own infinitesimal individual impression to the footprint that it leaves. Will the life-ore from which my feet, my daughter's feet – everyone's feet – are forged still issue in any footprint we would recognize as human a million years from now?

I'm not a foot fetishist. But at an aesthetic, symbolic, and perhaps spiritual level too, I've always found bare feet curiously moving. They have an air of ungainly innocence that hands never possess. They seem to carry with them a sense both of our vulnerability and toughness; they speak eloquently of the nature of the journey we are on. Sometimes when I hold my daughter's feet I can almost feel again their tiny newborn form. And I can imagine them cold and still, the feet on an old woman's body, her coffin carried by children whose embryonic feet budded within her, as hers did within her mother, as mine did within mine in the repeated repertoire of humanness we follow.

Despite the particularity of her feet, the fact that they're grounded in who she is, in who I am, despite the intensely focused specificity of this singular moment sitting on my knee, and all the equally particular moments that had to happen to give rise to it, her feet also have a sense of being in flux. This sense of flux stems from the knowledge that beside all our steps there are the paths we might have taken. Our stories are woven out of countless contingencies and choices. Rather than being immovably fixed in the precise grid of twists and turns that constitute our history, there's a sense that – with just a feather-light nudge – what happens to us, the experiences we embrace, the events that befall us, could have been completely different. Beating in the familiar warmth of my daughter's feet, as they are at this moment, I can also feel the strong pulse of potential, alternative, the many routes she might take closely shadowing the ones she has and will. Knowing how various are the paths that we can follow, how much we're at

the mercy of the accidental, how closely catastrophe and contentment run beside each other, makes me fearful. I hold my daughter's feet in wonder and with worry, thinking about what patterns they'll tread, to what places they'll take her, what other feet will lay their weight upon the ground beside her.

~

An observation of Paul Auster's struck me so much when I first heard it that I've committed his words to memory. They're spoken by Auggie Wren, one of the characters in the 1995 film *Smoke*, for which Auster wrote the screenplay:

> People say you have to travel to see the world. Sometimes I think that if you just stay in one place and keep your eyes open, you are going to see just about all that you can handle.

Auggie (played by Harvey Keitel) owns a small tobacconist's shop in Brooklyn, New York. The film focuses on a diverse group of his customers. The shop acts as a kind of narrative hub. It's touched by numerous storylines, which intermingle like threads of smoke. One of the ways in which Auggie 'keeps his eyes open' is by taking a photograph of the same street-view every day. He's been doing this for fourteen years. Studying the images makes him attentive to unsuspected seams of interest running through what, at first glance, appears tediously mundane and repetitive.

The idea that you don't have to travel far to see incredible things often comes to mind when I'm

Chris Arthur

Footnotes

holding my daughter's feet. Although it's fun to visit foreign places, you don't have to walk any great distance to see wonders and explore new vistas. All you need do is look down at your own feet and consider their nature – where they've come from, where they're going, the long walk that they're such a tiny part of. There are wonders – and terrors – wired into what seems entirely pedestrian. I would never have guessed before it happened that in the familiar circumstance of affectionately caressing my daughter's feet there could be so much unnerving strangeness. Sitting cheek-by-jowl with the little particularities of family life we know so well there are dwarfing anonymities of time and space and number. As we play 'this little piggy went to market' on our children's toes, seven billion other humans are alive, each one part of a lineage whose beginning and end we cannot see, each one walking on a planet that's just one minuscule part of a universe thought to have existed for fourteen billion years.

~

Auster's words often come to mind when I'm seeing my daughter off to school in the morning. She puts on her socks and shoes in the porch. I open the front door. We say our goodbyes and she walks down the drive, one foot following the other, her daily voyage out; stepping into her future. What could be more mundane, familiar, unremarkable? Yet it often leaves me with a sense of seeing just about all that I can handle.

This small parting as she goes to school – understated, ordinary – presages something vaster. A

foot holds in its familiar form the bloodline of the species; an everyday goodbye acts out in miniature the farewells implicit in our transience. As I stand at the door and watch her till she's out of sight, I know her steps are part of a journey that dwarfs her and that she's walking towards a moment when we'll say goodbye forever; when we'll move out of one another's sight and not come back. One moment will be the last time we exchange a smile; one touch will be the last one felt. My rogue meditation on feet touches the electricity of what it means to be alive – or so it feels – and the shock is jarring.

~

There are twenty-six bones in a human foot. How much that's written in their alphabet can we catch in the twenty-six letters that are the bones of language? The great Japanese haiku poet Matsuo Basho once said: 'Let not a hair's breadth separate your mind from what you write.' Words can't provide a perfect transcription of what we're thinking, let alone what's in the heart. I've tried to close to as narrow a space as I'm able the distance between what's written on these pages and what fills my mind with wonder and with love and anguish as I hold my daughter's feet. But I know there's far more than a hair's breadth between the experience and my attempt to record it. The gap is wide enough for much of what I think and feel to escape, leaving only a few remnants caught in these footnotes. They're like tattered pennants, regimental colours that help steel the spirit, marshal concentration; battle standards cut to ribbons in the struggle to understand the strangeness of our existence and the imponderables that face us.

Performance

Brian Cox

Trajectories

"I always remember that feeling of gratification that came from the response I got from my performance."

Unlike most people, I've always known what I wanted to do and I feel blessed in that. That goes back to childhood, standing on the bunker in my tenement home in Dundee, and my dad making me sing Al Jolson songs from when I was three and I always remember that feeling of gratification that came from the response I got from my performance. That, I suppose, was the lynchpin; I always had an instinct that I would go into this business, though I had no idea how I would do it. My circumstances play into this. I had a reasonably happy childhood, but my father died when I was eight and my mother was hospitalised with a series of nervous breakdowns. I was on my own and realised I'd have to cope. I was lucky in having wonderful sisters, but they were much older than me. I was born in nineteen forty-six, so in terms of age we were separated by a war.

Schooling for me was basically a disaster mainly because I got no parental help. I failed my 'eleven-plus'. I was taught by Maris Brothers initially. I went to St Mary's Forebank Primary School and they were great, but I lost my pals when they all went off to the housing schemes that sprung up in 1950s Dundee, so I was on my own in that respect too. We stayed in town when the rest were moving away from the centre of the city because my father owned a shop in Charles Street, just off the Wellgate. It was more than a shop; it was a social hub too, and he was a very generous man who gave out credit to his customers. When he died many didn't pay their debts and that was instrumental in my mother's ails; that and losing her husband when he was just fifty-one.

Brian Cox

Trajectories

"It seemed natural to me that acting was what I was going to do and the only question was how I was going to do it."

People remember my father to this day as being a kind of saintly man; losing him in my formative years in many ways shaped my future.

The school became more secular. Mr Robinson, the teacher, used to send me errands so I wasn't doing much schooling. 'Cox', he would say, 'I want you to nip down to Largs [the music shop] and pick up styluses for my gramophone.' I'd be sent down around 10 o'clock and I'd just wander round Dundee before I went back. I remember the Sasparilla Shop in the Overgate, Nelson's it was called, and I'd go there. So that was my life. I was almost playing at being a schoolboy, but I had the art of communication and that's what I could do. I went to the Secondary at St Michaels. It was Bill Dewar, the teacher, who introduced me to the Rep Club and we used to go there on a Wednesday after school. That introduced me to live acting. I already had a huge experience of cinema, because I went so often to every cinema in Dundee. That was a real part of me; in fact it was my heritage. Twice I had literally to break out of the Green's Playhouse, once seeing *Giant*, and once seeing *Hell on Frisco Bay*, and my sister went daft because I was missing. She had the police out looking for me, but I'd fallen asleep in the cinema. That was my life and it still is. My favourite Channel when I go home to the States is Turner Classic Movies.

It seemed natural to me that acting was what I was going to do and the only question was how I was going to do it. A series of fortuitous circumstances set things in action. A guy called Frank McDermott (everybody called him 'Fronk'), the brother of a classmate of mine, was giving up his job at the Rep to go to drama school in Glasgow; Bill Dewar, my teacher, suggested I should go for his job. I went and met John Henderson who was then director of the theatre – he was a New Zealander, Jewish, lame in one leg, and a really lovely man – and one of the questions he asked was whether I liked classical music. By luck I'd had a class in school the previous week which was on *Aida* so I promptly replied that I liked Verdi a lot. I got the job and I was made assistant to Bunty Kidd, the secretary. I was paid four pounds and ten shillings a week, ran errands, and washed the floor after performances every night – that was my first full-time job and it was in 1961. Eventually they let me backstage where I became the worst stage-manager ever. I loved it and practically lived there.

The old Rep burned down on my birthday, June 1st 1963. I tried to get in to help because it was virtually my home, but it was lost and I then moved to work with Ronnie Coburn in the Palace in Dundee. By this time I was being given a few small parts and I was acknowledged to have some talent. I remember us having a couple of directors, Tony Page and Piers Haggart, who helped me, but when Bill Davies came along, a Canadian who had been at LAMDA [London Academy of Music and Dramatic Arts], he brought up his voice teacher to help with a production of *Uncle Vanya*. This was a woman called Kristin Linklater, sister of Magnus and daughter of Eric Linklater, and she was one of the greatest ever voice-teachers. Through her I went to LAMDA; she went off to the States soon after but she came

back to teach in Kirkwall and is still there. My career then was heading toward stage acting, but my aspirations always revolved around screen performance. I disliked the exclusivity of theatre at that time in terms of their audiences, but I did like the inclusivity of being a part of things. My first working day was memorable; I saw a fisticuffs fight going on between Nicol Williamson, the actor, and Jeremy Fry, the stage manager; yet, at the same time, people were stepping over them and calling each other 'darling'. It was an interesting baptism for me.

The Rep was a great introduction. I would watch and work with actors from different schools and backgrounds, and it seemed to me the most philosophical style of drama teaching was given at LAMDA so that's where I applied to and went. Nowadays, somebody like me, from my background and circumstances, couldn't go there, but in the Sixties there was great social mobility, something that hasn't been seen since. I got a grant from our Education Authority; it was a full grant plus subsistence. I opted for London over Glasgow because Glasgow was, still is, quite alien to me because I'm an East-coaster. Kristin, my voice teacher, was in London, and I needed help to learn to speak, so you might call it destiny. I've always believed in destiny. I've always believed in following your instincts and I've always had goals to aim for. This kept me in good stead for the first ten years, but I also always accepted that I was in it for the long haul. And I've kept to that to the extent that I'm working harder now than I've ever worked. My gift is that I've always known where I wanted to go – I don't know

Brian Cox

Trajectories

"The one thing that grieves me about this University, about universities as a whole, is that I don't believe in the Lecture Hall. Nothing can better 'the conversation' and I firmly believe it's the best way to learn."

where that came from because I'm from such mixed Irish and Scottish stock, but it must be in the genes somewhere. I really believe that this town, and my Irish forebears who came here in the mid-1860s – and they were mainly women – have shaped me.

LAMDA gave me a fabulous grounding; it taught me how to read a play. The one thing that grieves me about this University, about universities as a whole, is that I don't believe in the Lecture Hall. Nothing can better 'the conversation' and I firmly believe it's the best way to learn. All the best teaching is done in small groups, and I would have loved this place to adopt that practice more. I feel some students fall through the gaps, because they're only involved maybe two or three hours a week; in Drama School you work on your body, and voice and you work 24/7. It's a hard regime, and you can't wing it. You can't 'not do' the work. It's not difficult to set yourself bars, but maintaining them is harder.

After LAMDA I was again lucky; I was auditioned by Tom Fleming when he was starting the Royal Lyceum. I was a kid and did my audition in the Steiner Hall in London. I was given the job. I was a bit raw but it put me in touch with my Scottishness. At the Rep I felt I'd been going through the motions, but this was different and was opening a matter of identity, of my identity, and that seemed to be, for Scottish actors, a mixture of vaudeville and straight – Duncan McRae comes to mind. It's Stanley Baxter, it's Fulton Mackay, it's Roddy McMillan, all great comedians yet also great straight actors. I worked with these characters, and it was an amazing education. However, I knew it was limiting and I didn't want this stereotypical Scottish label so I went to Birmingham next. I played all kinds of classic roles; the only one denied to me was *Hamlet* and that I always wanted to do. Those were the days when there was still proper Rep. By the age of 22, I was playing *Othello* and *Peer Gynt* and loving it. I had flashes of brilliance, and equal flashes of mediocrity, but this was learning your trade in the best way. This was the sixties, this was the best time to be alive, and by the age of 22 I was already comparatively experienced.

I married. Part of this was because the sixties were hedonistic times, drinking and a degree of debauchery, but I didn't need any of these excesses, especially from my background, so with stability, I was more concerned with my work. I remember working with Lindsay Anderson and having a great time with him. I was also working with the great Michael Elliot and my career was unfolding as it should unfold. I was very conscious of that and I was blessed – very blessed. The advantage I had in being an orphan was that you were always looking for that mentor, and I was fortunate in meeting so many. I used to actively pursue them – people like Fulton. The stage kept me gripped, yet, always, the world of the movie felt like a magnet. English film at that time bored me, and it was not until *Saturday Night and Sunday Morning* came along that I felt a revival of interest. I saw Albert Finney in that film in the Plaza in Dundee when I was fourteen and it was like a light switch. Seeing him, I reckoned that it was

all possible. He had this common-man quality, this alpha-male trait, and this wasn't around in American movies at that time: breaking down the class thing in performance. So did Tom Courtenay by the way.

In 1980 I did a TV thing with Finney about the Pope. But there was a real-life assassination attempt on the Pope at the time so it fell through and I was frustrated. On taking stock I realised how much I'd achieved – I'd played opposite Gielgud and other greats – at the age of thirty-one, but my thoughts were, 'where do I go from here?' I remember going up to Manchester to take over from Patrick McGoohan in *Moby Dick* because he didn't want to have his leg strapped up behind his back – he was 56 and I was 36 – and it was hard but great to do. Then I did two plays in London, one of them was with Glenda Jackson, both of which took me to Broadway and there I was spotted for my first movie part and I realised that my future would be in that direction. At this point, however, my marriage broke up and I came back here. We had married very early – I was 21 and she was 22. I joined the Royal Shakespearean Company, which was the last thing I thought I'd ever do, and began to play some excellent classic roles and kind of forgot the movie stuff. However, at the age of 49 I decided to get more serious about movies; I'd done *Braveheart* and other things, but I wanted more.

By the nineties I was doing more television, but most of the stuff was crap I thought. 'If I'm going to do crap I might as well get paid well for doing

Brian Cox

Trajectories

it'. The nineteen were barren years for quality in the Arts. So I went to the States, but then was tempted back by the offer of Masterclasses with the BBC along with Richard Wilson and Prunella Scales. In the middle of these, I received a phone call out of the blue asking me if I could be in Toronto the next day to do a film called *The Long Kiss Goodnight* because Dustin Hoffman, who was to play the part, was unable to do it. I did it and spent ten gruelling but brilliant days on it. I was doing the next show with Richard when the phone went again to ask if I could be in Chicago that Friday. Tommy Lee Jones had walked off this movie and they wanted me. I did it. I realised my destiny was moving to the movies. I knew these were going to be supporting parts, but I was happy to accept these. I remember speaking to the late lamented Nigel Hawthorn about this and he said he couldn't accept that sort of role; yet I remember him doing all sorts of these when he was climbing the ladder. In my early fifties I decided to pursue this earnestly. I made over a hundred movies since, and I came to understand that at times in a career, or in a life for that matter, there are risks and chances to be taken.

I believe that you have to keep challenging yourself, re-invent yourself. So I suppose instead of pursuing typical career trajectories, I've taken on 'Brian Cox' trajectories which are totally individual to me. George Danton famously said, 'He does what does him good', and that's what I strive to do. I'll be seventy soon and still feel I have things to do. I took on the Rector role at the University of Dundee for just such reasons. At first I thought it might be to the detriment of my work, but, actually, this was not the case. It allowed me to take another trajectory, doing different work whilst fulfilling my sense of commitment to education, to students and to this dear town. This was a case of me doing what did me good.

I'm sure the six-year-old me who used to perform for his parents would look at me now and consider that it all made sense. Of course there have been high points and low points, but there has always been a kind of sense to it and I feel incredibly blessed. I was given a vision, a sense of voyage, when I was a kid that has served me extraordinarily well.

Poetry

Lindsay Macgregor

Outset

She knew from the start that
their points of departure would differ.

He'd sail from Discovery Quay
on an ice-cutter bound for Antartica
with unshaven men who cut cards
and perished the thought of their fathers.

She'd leave the place
she called home in Peep o Day Lane
to walk with the women
for causes which couldn't be won
without staying and leaving at once.

Poetry

Lindsay Macgregor

Sweet Alice Canyon

They'd warned her
         not to walk
                 down there
                       where only
                           sharp-shod
                               mules should tread,
                                     beyond the boundless
                                         rim.
                                 But
                            she'd lain
                         dormant
                  long enough,
             heard talk of
       mammoth tracks
     near cataracts,
old ripple marks.
She picked
     her way on hard-packed
         trails, past
           unraked coals of trappers'
               camps, through
                 clouds of moose
                     flies
                  in the pinyon
            pines. Watched
         water disappear
       before her eyes,
     saw deserts form,
   heard junipers
  cut off
their limbs
   to save
     themselves from burdens
       even shamans
         couldn't bear.
.settle to silt the Allowed .nerve her held she nights cold bone Eight
Hunted shallows for tell-tale signs of baling buckets, mooring lines.

Biology

Ron Hay

Circuitous Routes

"As it turned out, it was in a department of Brewing and Biochemistry. That was what got me into science."

I had no idea what I wanted to do when I finished school. I was brought up and went to school in Dundee. I can remember sitting with a friend of mine, Ian, and we were leafing through university prospectuses. We came across a picture of a mini-brewery in the Heriot-Watt prospectus. We looked at it and said, 'That's absolutely brilliant! Let's go!' So we both applied and we both went to Heriot-Watt. As it turned out, it was in a department of Brewing and Biochemistry. That was what got me into science.

Arsenic is a simple element and it's abundant – you can get it virtually anywhere by just digging it out of the ground. It has metallic qualities but it's not a metal and because it can bind and interact with metals, it's used in gold extraction and it has many other industrial applications. It's been known as a treatment – for syphilis, cancer, for whitening the skin, and as a tonic - for thousands of years. Confucius and Hippocrates both wrote of its properties. But it was also a murderer's poison of choice for centuries when it couldn't be detected in the body. And in India, long-term exposure to arsenic in contaminated drinking water is harmful, even deadly, to millions of people to this day.

After I graduated from Heriot-Watt, the Medical Research Council Virology Unit in Glasgow had a place available. Somebody had dropped out so I took the place. That really set me on the path that I'm on just now. From there, I went to Harvard then I returned to Dundee via Glasgow and St. Andrews Universities. I was at St. Andrews for twenty years. In 2005 I moved here when they

Ron Hay
Circuitous Routes

"That's the amazing step he made. He was smart enough to realise that everyone who was cured so remarkably, had the same type of disease."

built the James Black Centre. This is a much bigger operation. I brought everybody here. It was an easy move. We were basically doing experiments one day in St. Andrews and we continued them here the next day. It couldn't have been easier.

A field doctor in rural North-West China was treating patients who had leukaemia, using traditional medicine of yellow ore which he dug out of the ground and mixed with mercury. He noted that while most of his patients died, there was a small group of patients who survived. That's the amazing step he made. He was smart enough to realise that everyone who was cured so remarkably, had the same type of disease. Apparently, the clinical features of this cancer are obvious because patients have a very pronounced bleeding; there are problems with platelets and clotting. In a hospital here, they would just take some cells and extract the DNA and do a simple diagnostic test. He didn't have access to that. He was able to see that they all had a related syndrome. He wrote up his findings which were picked up by Zhu Chen, a haematologist in Shanghai. Zhu Chen and his team demonstrated that the form of leukaemia which responded to treatment was Acute Promyelocytic Leukaemia (APL). He isolated the active ingredient, arsenic trioxide, purified it, and trialled the treatment with similar success. Initially, reports that 95% of patients were completely cured were met with some scepticism in the West until they were replicated here.

Several allopathic medicines derive from traditional medicines – aspirin from willow bark, tamoxifen (used in breast cancer treatment) from yew, for example. Laboratories try to sift out those which may have scientifically-provable efficacy. But that's no easy task. The molecule which has effect may be very complicated and therefore difficult for chemists to work with: they have to be able to synthesise it or make it in large quantities. It's also very difficult to control for the placebo effect which is by no means fully understood. There's a lot of things which are just superstition, but it's also absolutely clear that there's a lot to be gleaned from traditional medicine.

In the normal evolution of cells, they begin life as undifferentiated. Then they proliferate and differentiate; the proliferation stops and differentiation continues. These cells have a fixed life span of around two weeks – they do their work, then die. But in their diseased state, they continue to proliferate. In APL, two genes fuse. The Promyelocytic Leukaemia (PML) gene fuses with the gene encoding the retinoic acid receptor alpha. That's the flaw in the system. That's the thing which actually causes the disease. The two genes that are fused together block the process of differentiation so they become stuck at the stage where they just continue to proliferate. Other cancers, particularly solid tumours, are different.

Serendipity starts with an unexpected observation. There's a particular problem you would like to solve. You then formulate a hypothesis and design experiments to test that hypothesis. And you try to test that as rigorously as possible to see if it's true.

And often what happens is that when you're in the process of doing this, you get a result which completely puzzles you. And you say, 'Not only does it not prove the hypothesis but it probably suggests the hypothesis is completely wrong.' Initially, when you start out in science, there's disappointment when you can't prove the hypothesis. The longer you're in science, you realise that this is when you make the real discoveries. Because if you can predict pretty much how everything is going to be, you've probably not learned very much. It's easy to have a blinkered view of things. You have to guard against believing something without the evidence for it. That's faith rather than science. The way to do science is to test the hypothesis and design good experiments. If they don't give you the expected result, they still give you a result. It's worked. The result is the result. You don't change that. That's how it is. It's good if you can say, 'Well, that hypothesis was wrong.' People can get attached to a particular hypothesis – that's one of the worst things that can happen in science. You've got to dissociate yourself and your ego from the idea and the hypothesis.

In APL, the solution is to get rid of cancer stem cells because usually normal therapy will kill most of the tumour or replicating cells but you can still be left with these stem cells which can go on to repopulate the host. They tend to be difficult to kill with standard therapeutics. But if you can kill the stem cells, that's thought to be curative. Arsenic not only kills the proliferating cancer cells but it also kills the cancer stem cells. It does both in one go. This is why it's thought to be so remarkably effective. It's an amazing story.

Ron Hay

Circuitous Routes

We heard about the arsenic story. Our involvement was to try to figure out what arsenic actually does. It's an unusual job for us. It's different from how we usually work – usually we say, 'Here's the problem. Develop the drug'. In this case, it's 'Here's the drug. How does it work?' In this case the treatment for the disease is already available and what we would like to do is understand, at the molecular level, how it works such that people with APL can now go to Out Patients for arsenic injections which in the main cure them of cancer? If we can understand how arsenic works, we hope that we can use arsenic therapy to cure other leukaemias.

The frontline method of treatment in hospitals virtually everywhere nowadays is very low doses of arsenic, below toxic levels. People have fewer side effects with arsenic than they do with conventional chemotherapy. The advantage of injection is that a lot of the toxicity with arsenic is through the liver – it kills liver cells – so if you inject people, it avoids a route going straight to the liver. So the concentration when it actually gets to the liver is so much lower. And because leukaemia is a sort of blood cancer, the cells are in the blood, so you inject directly into the circulation. The arsenic hits the cells that it needs to hit.

When I look at the people I've had in the lab who've been really successful, they're all smart but not necessarily geniuses. I think it's experimental rigour that characterises those that make important discoveries. It takes a lot of patience and you've got to have a pretty high boredom threshold because there's a lot of stuff you do that

is very repetitive. Sometimes if people are too smart, it just doesn't work very well in science. They can't knuckle down to grinding through the experiments because they're off thinking about the next great idea. Really good people have good ideas, but they've also got the ability to just knuckle down. It takes hard graft and careful observation.

The two-gene fusion in PML is effectively blocking the cells from differentiating. When the arsenic degrades it, you remove the block. And so all these cells then differentiate as normal. But then, amazingly, they also die just as they would normally have done. That gets rid of the whole clone of cells which has the mutation. The beauty of the arsenic-based leukaemia treatment is that it kills not only the proliferating cancer cells but also the stem cells at the root of the problem, by inducing degradation in the oncogenic fusion protein.

Because of the way arsenic targets things, we may be able to use it in other cancers – to try to get it to target other stem cells. It clearly does kill stem cells in general. It's at a very early stage. Here in Dundee, we chanced on it because we were working on PML for other reasons. I think the intellectual side of it is absolutely fascinating. We still don't actually understand what arsenic does to this PML protein. This involves getting into basic structural biology. We've got a drug that's effective, but we've no idea how it works.

Art and Science are not so different. Imagination is used in both. Both take an innovative idea and convert it into something. The processes are similar, even in the training; to be a great painter, there's a huge amount of skill you just have to learn. People see things differently who've done great art and some of the really great scientists are the same. Einstein saw something that other people couldn't see – it was incredibly innovative and new and the best art is like that as well. What you end up doing can be quite different from what you set out to do.

Scientific writing must describe results as accurately as possible. It differs from creative writing in that way. We don't want to be too creative. There is a message to get across. We collect data. We describe what is in each figure. We don't want too many words. We don't want any ambiguity. The discussion can be a bit more creative. But it's formulaic writing. You have to have accuracy.

The path to new discoveries is often not a straight one. We've not worked on the same thing all the time. Some of it has just come down to serendipitous discoveries. That is one of the things I always try and tell new students is that the thing you've got to look out for is the unexpected findings; you must have an open mind about how you deal with them because you never know where they're going to take you. I think the important thing in science these days is to be flexible. You don't want to put yourself in a box and say, 'I only do this sort of thing.' You've really got to have an open mind.

There are real eureka moments when you look at something and immediately realise that this reveals a tremendous insight. It's a fantastic feeling. There are moments when you've been trying to do something and suddenly it just works. Literally things crystalize – sometimes you can try for years, you look down and there are crystals in the plate. It can take years of nothing doing, then one day you look down and it's happening. That's a beautiful moment. That's the enjoyment of the lab. The resolution. The conclusion.

Kim Kremer

The Coin Testers

"The essay is the purest form of education because it is not concerned only with facts but with ideas"

In 1949, Tom Kremer was serving in the Israeli army in Tel Aviv. He had survived the concentration camp of Bergen Belsen, left his home country of Hungary and missed out on over four years of schooling. He was nineteen years old. There was a paucity of books in the army camp, but a few were passed hand to hand. One of these books was written in Hebrew by the Zionist writer, Ahad Ha'am; the effect of his words stayed with Tom for the rest of his life:

> Every civilised man who is born and bred in an orderly state of society lives all his life in the condition of the hypnotic subject, unconsciously subservient to the will of others…. Language and literature, religion and morality, laws and customs – all these and their like are the media through which society puts the individual to sleep, and constantly repeats to him its commandments.[1]

Ahad Ha'am believed that only very occasionally the 'breath of a new spirit' knocks at the door and wakes us from our hypnotic slumber. Tom was struck by the power of Ha'am's ideas, his own beliefs suddenly thrown into uncertainty. This was his first encounter with the essay, and created in him a life-long passion for the form. In the absence of formal schooling, Tom educated himself by reading essays.

The essay, writes Tom now, 'is the purest form of education because it is not concerned only with facts but with ideas. Ahad Ha'am remains for me the pinnacle of the essayist's achievement. His writing is illuminated by a single, original idea and he leads you by the nose to his devastating conclusion. He is usually referred to as the founder of Zionism, but he should be famous as a great essayist.'

Tom went on to spend most of his working life in business until, at the age of eighty, he decided to found Notting Hill Editions, a press with a single driving aim: to revive the art of the essay. Amongst its publications is *Words of Fire*, a little-known selection of Ahad Ha'am's essays.

This year the company will celebrate its fifth birthday. Recently, my father, Tom, and I took time to sit down together to talk about the early beginnings of NHE. 'I wondered why no-one seemed to write essays anymore,' he said, explaining his reasons for beginning the enterprise. 'Why has it become unpopular?'

Squeezed out perhaps by the rise of the novel, and the flood of newspapers and long form articles, it seems as if the precious essay has dwindled, existing in a narrow space between fiction and non-fiction. But what made him think people would be interested in revising such an idea? 'You have only to say the word *essay* and people respond – "ah, the essay?" and you can see them instantly recalling their personal experience of reading them. It creates an emotional response – sometimes a negative response, but there is always this spark of curiosity.'

His mission would be to root out the true essays, and give them a home with NHE. Readers would begin to turn to the form again, he was sure, because it is the place where ideas can be experimented with and questioned in their most essential form. Yet defining an essay is as elusive as mercury – just when you think you've got it, it slips through your fingers. What exactly is meant then, by *essay*? 'It is, crucially, not to be confused with the academic essay; it is not concerned with facts, or with peer review or with collating the opinions of others. On the contrary, a true essayist thinks what no-one else is thinking. That's the whole point. A distinctive voice, but also one with a sense of intimacy. The essayist draws you near, as though you were having a conversation by the fireside. It is not the impersonal voice of the scholar. And ideally, it should have a central idea that brings all the surrounding elements towards it, illuminating the whole.'

Notting Hill Editions would have two strands to its publishing. The main trunk of the publishing would be the classic essays by some of the greatest practitioners of the form, such as Hazlitt, Virginia Woolf, Montaigne and Ahad Ha'am. Its branches would be grown by new writers, stretching and playing with its form. After all, by its nature, the essay is experimental. But whether old or new, every work should be aimed at, as Virginia Woolf remarked, the 'common reader'. Tom says, 'I imagine the reader sinking into an armchair by the fire with one of our books in hand. But when she has finished reading it, she will not be the same person on getting up from the chair as she was when she sat down.' But what is this quality that makes the reader get up from the chair a changed person?

Kim Kremer

The Coin Testers

The film director Warner Herzog said in an interview that his documentary films aim for 'ecstatic truth'. In his 'Minnesota Declaration', he observed:

> 1. Cinéma vérité confounds fact and truth, and thus plows only stones. And yet, facts sometimes have a strange and bizarre power that makes their inherent truth seem unbelievable.
> 2. Fact creates norms, and truth illumination.[2]

This quality of finding something true is at the heart of the best essays, as it is in all great art. Art does not seek to make an exact replica of life, but to illuminate what we cannot see for ourselves. An essay is never purely factual, as non-fiction is. This, above all, is what defines the essay: *truth, not fact.*

And how does the essayist attain it? John Jeremiah Sullivan in his introduction to *Best American Essays* tries to define the true meaning of the word 'essay' in the way that Montaigne might have intended it; 'It's the sense of "a proofe, tryall, experiment." To test something—for purity, or value (going back to coinage; the *essayeur* was "an Officer in the Mint, who touches everie kind of new coyne before it be delivered out").'[3]

The essayist handles the truth of his ideas, testing them out on the page. The writer finds out what she thinks through the writing process itself, and like a charcoal sketch, may show her workings-out on the page. There are no slick certainties, no easy formula to follow. She may not know herself where she will end up when she begins.

The essayist picks beneath the surface, excavating the essential quality of thought that would pass the coin-tester's fingers. This is the hardest of tasks. J.B. Priestley understood this, when he wrote about the rigorous demands of essay writing over other forms of non-fiction:

> …to have nothing to cling hold of, to have no excuse for writing at all, to be compelled to spin everything out of oneself, to stand naked and shivering in the very first sentence one puts down, is clearly a very different matter, and this is the melancholy situation in which the essayist always finds himself.[4]

The essay has no borders. Phillip Lopate described it as 'shaggy'.[5] It is the most questioning and exploratory form of writing. It is not memoir or confessional, as Adam Mars-Jones remarked, whilst judging the 2015 Notting Hill Editions Prize, 'the essay must not only exist in the deep trenches of the self' although these might be part of it. The difference between a memoirist and an essayist is that the essayist looks outward, and attempts to translate their feelings into a universal language. In doing so, this adventurer in language and ideas discovers not only himself, but a piece of the world, a part of the great *out there* of thought.

Poetry

Dundee International Women's Centre*

last lines

there is no word for   first light
it's more like   *find yourself*

study   -   play   -   talk to the other
come back in the same way
arrive at the night   in an army town

did I know I'd leave before I knew?

my heart is still on my country road
            small fish and smoke
bokharat   kapsa   cardamom   jackfruit
        honey cake   apple cake
father's farm of rice and sweet potatoes

what is in your suitcase? it seems so heavy
your name?   your family?   your country?
someone's always choosing for us

leaving the shade of Lakshmi's green dome, walking
across a field of white birds and blueberries
we forget the hard thing happened
find our balance

* Contributors:
Amandine
Amandeep
Balgeis
Lindsay
Madhuri
Magda
Maria
Mashael
Mei
Rekha

Essay

Alison Donnell

Lifelines

"In the 1990s, when I started out in academia, it was the commonplace protocol to 'position' oneself. Talks often began with a pointed disavowal or a freighted apology, 'as a white, middle-class woman scholar…' I never felt comfortable with that."

Having studied, delighted in, puzzled over and praised Caribbean Literature for the best part of thirty years, the West Indies feels like an unremarkable place for me to belong in my mind. And yet as a white British woman born to a Midlands industrial landscape, the strangeness of my long and intense connection to the Caribbean archipelago is never lost on others. It is a genuinely rare moment when a first conversation about my research specialism doesn't provoke the question 'And, tell me, what connects you to the Caribbean?' There is no earlier connection that I know of forged deep in my blood or double-helix and yet I can see their disappointment when I say 'books'.

Despite my defiantly anti-identitarian principles, I can of course see why being white and British prompts that query. In the 1990s, when I started out in academia, it was the commonplace protocol to 'position' oneself. Talks often began with a pointed disavowal or a freighted apology, 'as a white, middle-class woman scholar…' I never felt comfortable with that. It wasn't that I was unaware of what it meant to be all of those things, that I hadn't already had many experiences that taught me to feel the weight of whiteness as privilege, to recognise all the advantages that a middle-class life and upbringing brought with it, as well as a smaller number of negative confrontations on account of my gender. Even then, what was most rewarding and vital about my work were encounters and connections that couldn't be adequately prefaced by an 'as a…': giddying ways of thinking that sent the clarity and stability of such positionings into a spin. I didn't consider myself outside/beyond/above my work but rather the work I did insistently challenged and changed the way I thought about identities altogether. Such safe footholds were not available and the thrill of the journey was to find a way to hold on in a more slippery, unfamiliar terrain.

From early on, what I had come to cherish about my encounters with Caribbean peoples and places was the possibility of thinking differently about how identities multiply, how their shapes of animation shift and also how the structures kept rigid by historical conviction started to unravel at the edges. Working at being a Caribbeanist involved opening myself to the marvelous prolif-eration of ancestries, ethnicities and attachments both across and within communities and individuals. It wasn't that I was avoiding those vexed issues around skin, race and history when I chose not to preface my papers, it was just that I was wrestling with what it meant, and what it might do to declare an identity in that way, including a fraudulent idea of racial awareness that cost nothing.

Looking back now, for me the fraudulent feeling was focused on what I knew, not who I was. I worked hard to be sure that I would have something to say. I was nervous being around other students who had clearly grown up in bookish homes, friends whose parents had PhDs, and tutors who were (gulp!) personal friends with writers. So while my journey to the Caribbean struck others as curious, even awkward, for me the crossing to a life devoted to books was the more unfamiliar and unpredictable one. My parents were both from working-class families

and had left school by the age of fifteen. Their intelligence and ambition could not be indulged outside paid employment and the sheer effort they both expended in continuing their education in the workplace was lost on me as a child, although their aspirations for my sister and me to enjoy education must have seeped through somehow since we both decided on a teaching career. And though we were not a family with books, we were a family with travels. When my engineer father returned from business trips in Japan, America and Germany we would race to unpack his suitcase which always had a culinary treat tucked between his crumpled shirts. From pungent chewy seaweed that made us pull fish faces to saccharine sticky popcorn that we burnt but still ate in its silver foil pan, the heady combination of surprises, smells and stories was our way of sharing his journeys.

When my father took up a job in India, I needed to find a place to study. I had a dread of private schools – especially the all-girl variety – and applied to Atlantic College as purely a pragmatic decision. I had no idea of the extraordinary nature of this international boarding school with an insistently broad curriculum and an equally insistent philosophy of international understanding infused by the teachings of its founder, the peace philosopher Kurt Hahn. I had joined the college intent on continuing my social life and preparing for a medical degree. However, the life stories I encountered there, the compulsory course in theories of knowledge and a truly inspirational literature teacher, Catherine Jackson, changed my direction of travel. I left for university wanting to

Alison Donnell

Lifelines

enter the fray over meaning and to discover more about the work that words could do in the world. My parents were still in India and my sister in France when I headed to the leafy, white tile campus of the University of Warwick in my homeland of Midlands England. I was not far from Coventry – possibly the least glamorous place in Europe – where I had also been born. But, in my second year, when I took a special option on Caribbean Literature taught by the Guyanese critic Michael Gilkes, my voyage began. Excited, engrossed and enlivened, I was encouraged to speak about ethnicity and gender, about an ethics of representation and a politics of style. The works he selected were creatively brilliant but their luminosity was also enhanced by their ability to make me think about transformative meaning, of what is at stake when we represent the lives of others.

As the first person in my family to go to university, my journey to a PhD was entirely unmapped and unknown. I didn't know what a PhD was when Michael Gilkes and David Dabydeen suggested it to me. I can remember my father's look – both sceptical and proud. He didn't live to see me become a 'Dr' but I am sure he would have teased me about my failure to treat the family's disorders. My own worries niggled - where this was taking me and what I might do? Maybe I was being too bold, too expectant about the possibilities for travelling across worlds? I had discovered that books were vessels we can board in safety and privacy but being in the physical reality of the Caribbean was also part of my journey.

When I landed in Trinidad for my first research trip in the West Indiana collection at the St Augustine, it felt and smelt like India. That mottled terrain of the familiar and strange continued; the library rules were familiar but the interest of the staff in my work was certainly not. The botanical garden campus was familiar but the evening ballet packed with white Trinidadians – almost none of whom I had seen in shops, on buses or walking by – was not. The tiny ants were familiar (but unwelcome). The size and texture of avocados and mangoes was not (though welcome). I loved and still do love the heat and light of the tropics: the piquant bird pepper sauce that pinches, the picong tongue inducing often inappropriate but connecting laughter. My library days were broken when the news of CLR James's death came in. His funeral was to be held in Trinidad, not London where he had died. Kenneth Ramchand, who had been an important mentor to me, called to ask if I wanted to attend. My first reaction was that I could not possibly claim a place at such an important Trinidadian event. Ken replied quite directly, 'You are a white woman and my wife is a white woman. She cannot go and no one will know who you are. Do you want to come?' It was such an unexpected and frankly refreshing take on the 'as a white, middle-class woman scholar…' refrain. All that mattered was to get on with work and with colleagues. Attending the funeral was like being given cultural supplements intravenously and my memories of Lamming and Sparrow have never faded. Neither did the impact of Ken's simple disregard for my 1990s UK academy identity crisis.

For me these travels have been an ongoing necessity and education. Not being of the Caribbean, I needed to find ways to be in it. The desire to know what I didn't know, to read what I hadn't read, go where I hadn't been, listen to what I hadn't heard, and taste what I hadn't eaten has never diminished and never approached satisfaction. It may have been my need to prove to myself and my family that academic work was real work but I have reached deep into archives and libraries, the brains and the memories of colleagues, the curiosity of students, the goodwill of anyone I met who gave me reason to think they knew something about Caribbean Literature that I didn't. I have done so without anything as purposeful or ambitious as a voyage. No eye on a destination. The textbooks, companions and reference works I have edited have been the workings out of my inner journeys, always incomplete, always leading to a magnified sense of what I was yet to learn.

I co-edited *The Routledge Reader in Caribbean Literature* when I was straight out of my PhD. I had a yearning to see the bigger picture but that project could only have happened so effortlessly on account of my extraordinary naivety. Thirty years later, I am about to embark on a three volume critical study of Caribbean Literature for Cambridge University Press and, because I know so much more, the task feels so much harder. I am paralyzed by the choices because I now recognise that I am not just learning aloud on paper. When Marlon James's *Brief History of Seven Killings* became the book of the season, lots of people commented on the irony of the word 'brief' in the title of an almost 700 page book. No such thought ever occurred to me; the long history of the Caribbean stretches back centuries as do the narratives of cross-cultural interference and exchange and the extraordinary tradition of linguistic propensity and inflammation that James's book taps into.

The more I have travelled the longer the journey ahead appears to be. When a few years ago I was awarded a research fellowship with the rare privilege of time and funds to spend in the Caribbean, I ached for an extended voyage. I had long yearned to busy myself by day in the archives and then stretch my mind and body along the edge of blue water, waiting patiently for that green flash of inspiration. But my mother's decline – her Parkinson's disease and dementia by now quite advanced – meant that she could no longer travel with me and sleep soundly at the back of lecture theatres, or reach for my hand under the table at meals when the conversation b-ecame too uncomfortably academic. I could not be away for more than a couple of weeks. My open suitcase sat at the end of my bed in Cheltenham, Reading, Kingston, Trois Islets, Port of Spain, Russia Gully, Grand Anse... Clothes and books were half-packed and unpacked for ten trips that year as I voyaged in and out of my world of work, an emotional haven where I could be functional, effective and optimistic. The first row of economy seats on Virgin Atlantic became one of the places where it felt natural, comfortable to be. Unremarkably but consciously occupying the space between now familiar places claimed by both intellectual industry and emotional intimacy, I held on to my books and waited for the physical relief I knew would come as they reminded me, unprompted, what it is that literature does – it moves us.

Kim Adamson & Wendy Gammie

The story of RRS *Discovery*

"a man with 'imagination and enthusiasm... be calm, yet quick and decisive in action"

At the beginning of the twentieth century Antarctica was still an uncharted wilderness. Exploration was a daunting task, involving a long voyage through remote and tempestuous seas just to reach the continent. The 1901 British National Antarctic Expedition was the product of the vision of Sir Clements Markham, President of the Royal Geographical Society. Naturally cautious, Markham saw the aims of the expedition as purely scientific. Being the first to reach the South Pole was never one of the objectives. By 1900 Markham had raised the necessary funds, now all he needed was a ship, and a man to lead the expedition.

As a major whaling centre Dundee's shipyards had long experience of constructing ships robust enough to travel through the Arctic pack ice. It was this expertise that Markham harnessed to build RRS *Discovery*, the first vessel to be constructed specifically for scientific research. While the design was based on the great Dundee whalers, there were some modifications. Magnetic surveys were to be an important part of the scientific work of the expedition. To be sure of complete accuracy an exclusion zone round the magnetic observatory was created, with no iron or steel allowed within thirty feet of the area.

Markham wanted 'a naval officer in the regular line... young and a good sailor with experience of ships under sail', a man with 'imagination and enthusiasm... be calm, yet quick and decisive in action.'[1] The man he appointed was Lieutenant Robert Falcon Scott, a young naval officer he had first encountered twelve years earlier. Scott was appointed in June 1900 and promoted to Commander RN at the age of just 33. A rather shy man, he was also steady, strong and, as later events were to prove, immensely courageous.

Scott took personal charge of all preparations for the expedition. On 6th August, *Discovery* was finally ready, slipping her moorings at Cowes, on the Isle of Wight, to begin her epic journey. It was a journey not without incident. En-route to New Zealand the vessel was lashed by gales and high seas, throwing her around like a toy boat. Tragedy struck on departure from Lyttelton Harbour in New Zealand. A young seaman, Charles Bonner, fell from the main mast, hurtling headfirst to his death, his skull crushed on the iron deckhouse.

Forty-nine men started the journey south, each one hand-picked by Scott. Scientists apart, they were a mixture of merchant and naval seamen, a decision Scott came to regret as tensions broke out between the codes. As well as Scott, two other senior crewmembers stand out in particular: Ernest Shackleton and Edward Wilson. Despite being invalided home from his first visit to the Antarctic, Shackleton was obsessed with this bleak desert of ice. He was to return to the Antarctic three times including the ill-fated *Endurance* expedition that earned him a place in Polar history.

Scott had worked tirelessly to ensure no detail was overlooked. No one knew for how long the expedition would be cut off from the outside world. Everything had to be taken on board with them. Exhaustive provisions lists for three years were made – tropical and polar clothing, sledges, tents, furs, tools, explosives, signal rockets, a library of over a hundred books, lamps, candles, medicines and alcohol, described aptly as medical comforts! Many of the food stores were supplied free by firms with an eye on publicity – custard powder from Bird & Sons, lime juice from Evans, Lesher & Webb and two tons of Cocoa Powder from Cadbury's. As almost every man smoked, tobacco was vital so 1,000 lbs were duly stowed. Further stores were taken on board in New Zealand. On the day *Discovery* left, the deck was a melee of twenty three howling dogs, a flock of forty five terrified sheep (a gift from the farmers of New Zealand) all milling around countless packing cases, sacks of food and timber for huts. An extraordinary scene indeed.

After five months at sea, Antarctica was eventually sighted on January 8th 1902. The main purpose of the expedition was scientific – to make magnetic surveys and carry out meteorological, oceanographic, geological and biological research. Five scientists carried out the work: zoologist Edward Wilson, biologist Thomas Hodgson, geologist Hartley Ferrar, physicist Louis Bernacchi and the ship's senior surgeon and botanist Dr. Reginald Koettlitz. Hauling sledges through blizzards in temperatures as low as minus 45°, they risked frostbite and snow blindness to take measurements and collect specimens.

The work was truly groundbreaking. Over five hundred new kinds of marine animals, spiders, shrimps, star and shellfish were discovered. The expedition was the first to sight an Emperor

Kim Adamson & Wendy Gammie

The story of the RRS *Discovery*

penguin rookery and obtain an egg of the species. Many hundreds of miles of unknown coast, towering mountain ranges and glaciers were mapped. Invaluable magnetic measurements, auroral observations and seismic recordings were made. After the research had been analysed and the Royal Geographical Society came to publish the findings, ten large, weighty volumes resulted. This represented a major contribution to the understanding of the Antarctic continent, a feat made all the more remarkable considering the extreme conditions endured by the heroic scientists of *Discovery*.

On November 2nd 1902 Scott, Wilson and Shackleton set off to cross the Great Ice Barrier and explore the frozen desert beyond. With them were nineteen dogs pulling five sledges laden with 1,853 lbs of supplies and equipment. On November 25th they had passed latitude 80° south, charting new lands and features every day. But there was a heavy price to pay. One by one the under-nourished dogs began to die. The men too were beginning to suffer dreadfully. They carried on until December 30th, when, at latitude 82° 17', they reluctantly turned for home. Shackleton was in the advanced stages of scurvy, incapacitated and coughing up blood through his congested throat. Against near impossible odds they arrived back at *Discovery* on 3rd February 1903. They had trudged over 950 miles in 93 days, travelling further south than any man before them.

By December 1903 there was 20 miles of ice between *Discovery* and the open sea, with no apparent way out. On January 4th 1904 two

relief ships arrived, *Morning* and *Terra Nova*. Finally, on February 16th, controlled explosions were used to blow *Discovery* free from her icy prison and the expedition headed for home.

Landfall was made at Spithead on September 10th 1904 to a rapturous reception. Scott was acclaimed as a national hero and awarded numerous honours. RRS *Discovery*'s adventures continued, first with the Hudson Bay Company, then running munitions to Russia during the First World War. She was to make two further voyages to Antarctica before being laid up in London.

In 1925 *Discovery* set sail for the Southern Seas once again. The expedition's mission was to research whale stocks and their migration patterns thus providing a scientific basis for whaling industry regulation. As on Discovery's last trip south, important scientific breakthroughs were made. The expedition was crucial to our understanding of whales and ushered in the beginnings of conservation thinking.

The British, Australian and New Zealand Antarctic Expedition was *Discovery*'s third and final trip south. The brief on this trip was twofold: to chart the coastlines, islands, rocks and shoals between Queen Mary Land and Enderby Island and to 'plant the British Flag wherever... it [was] practicable to do so.'[2] Whole new lands were discovered and charted, and a mass of geological and zoological samples collected; territory was also added on behalf of the British Government.

In 1986, *Discovery* made her triumphant return to Dundee; this was to be her final berth.

Film

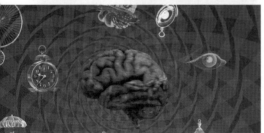

Gary Gowans

Axis Mundi: The Making of an Epic Short
Film

I was recently in John Mulligan's public bar in
Dublin, passing the time in some very creative
company, when someone asked, 'What are you
up to these days?'
'I'm making a short film.'
'Are you really?'
I'm acutely aware of the fact that anyone with a
smart phone can say that they are making a short
film, and I now find myself a little shy when
divulging this.
'What's it about?'
To hide my true earnestness I tried to be coy, and
a little self-mocking. 'It's an existential "sci-fi-los-
ophy" piece that investigates matters of life and
death, and the age-old ideological battle between
spirituality and science. It's
about a scientist who determines to visit God.'
Lots of laughter buoyed by lots of Guinness.

As descriptions go, my anecdote is meant to be a
little tongue-in-cheek. Designing a poster for the
film, I roughed out an alternative synopsis that
owes something to Douglas Adams: Dr William
Demarcus is a world-renowned scientific genius
who is singularly determined to unravel the mystery
of the *ultimate question of life, the universe, and
everything.* So where better to get his answer than
straight from the horses mouth? That will serve as
a placeholder for the moment.

The title of my film is *Axis Mundi* which, in
certain belief cultures, refers to the 'world centre'
or 'the bridge between heaven and earth.' The
story was originally inspired by a newspaper
article that reported on academic research into
'Near Death Experience' (NDE). The article

Gary Gowans

Axis Mundi: The Making of an Epic Short Film

highlighted incidents where people claim to have left their bodies and, from above, have observed their surroundings. Another commonly reported scenario involves the miraculous transportation to a different, unearthly plane – often through a bright tunnel or portal – to meet with an otherworldly spirit or deceased relatives. From a historical perspective, experiences of this nature have been recorded in works as diverse as *The Bible*, Plato's *Dialogues* and *The Tibetan Book of the Dead*, and by writers from Homer to Ernest Hemingway. Surprisingly, Homer Simpson has never experienced an NDE, but in Season 5, Episode 18 Mr Burns does! Opinions vary as to the cause of these phenomena. Scientists commonly attribute this to the lack of blood-flow and oxygen to the brain during extreme trauma; people who have experienced NDE are often more inclined towards spiritual or theological theories. Again the ideological battle lines are drawn.

My story is about a man, Dr William Demarcus, who, from a very young age, is lauded as a prodigy. A man of almost infinite academic ability, Demarcus is, in his twilight years, confronted by the idea that his life's work may come to nothing. We understand that he has been divorced several times and that he has sold his skills and talents to pursue the dream of ultimate knowledge. Dr Demarcus is not unlike Christopher Marlowe's Dr Faustus. My man is, naturally, an amalgam of cinematic boffin archetypes, from Dr Caligari, Dr Morbius and Professor Quatermass to Dr Henry Jones Senior and Dr Henry Jekyll. In case you think the intellectual air is thinning somewhat, it is worth noting that Dr Morbius – played by

Walter Pidgeon in MGM's science fiction classic *Forbidden Planet* (1956) – is essentially Prospero from William Shakespeare's *The Tempest*. It's true that nothing is original.

The film is, in part, a rumination on the nature of isolation and loneliness in later life and considers how this can arise through the kind of choices we make during our lifetime. Demarcus is something of an egotist (perhaps a not unjustified conviction), who clearly has a relationship with drink. His only other real relationship is with Juno, a computerised avatar administrator, who looks after all of his professional needs. The lines in their relationship are often blurred. This description makes Demarcus sound like a rather sad and unsympathetic character, but he is not without a sense of humour.

The film culminates in a voyage, a metaphorical – or perhaps metaphysical – voyage to, what Shakespeare has called, 'the undiscovered country'. Again, this is not the first time that Shakespeare has informed the plot of a sci-fi movie (see *Star Trek VI: The Undiscovered Country* (1991)). Demarcus' groundbreaking work in Neuroscience leads him to try to invent a machine that can read minds. And to quote Demarcus, 'that's when the military got interested.' His breakthrough moment comes when he realises that the machine only works on people experiencing an NDA. Following this discovery his research leads to a professional/spiritual crisis and an almost evangelical obsession with 'Die Neue Rettung' or 'The New Salvation'. He comes to believe that by experiencing a self-inflicted NDA while connected

Gary Gowans
Axis Mundi: The Making of an Epic Short Film

to his machine, he might be able to meet with God, uncover the truth of existence, and record a transcript of the interview.

The journey undertaken by Demarcus is an archetypal tale. Just like Jason, Demarcus builds his Argo to pursue his golden fleece. Much like biblical prophets, he wanders into the wilderness and climbs the mountain to meet with his God. Demarcus suggests that he is creating a capsule. Capsule does, of course, have two meanings: a vessel of transportation, like a space capsule, and a means of administering medication. Is Demarcus' journey real or is it the result of consuming a mind-altering substance? The capsule that he swallows before his voyage could be designed to chemically induce a near death experience, but it might equally be the case that he is using it to initiate a very different kind of 'trip'. His internal journey meets with the idea that 'The highest revelation is that God is in everyman' (Ralph Waldo Emerson). In the end it is left to the viewer to determine the true nature of Demarcus' experience. When we see him swallow the capsule and drink a magic elixir, the scene is reminiscent of a Holy Communion, where the scientist becomes the priest consuming the body and blood of Christ. He is surrounded by the saintly halo of the machine as he casts off on his voyage.

The meeting place for Demarcus' encounter with the infinite is influenced by the legends of the Ancient Sibyls. The Sybil of Cumae famously lived in a cave where she would read the auspices for the great and the good of Ancient Greece and Rome. The classical hero Aeneas consulted with the Cumaean Sibyl before his descent into the underworld. In Robert Graves' *I, Claudius*, the young *'Clau-Clau-Claudius'* meets with the prophetess to hear of his future prospects. When considering how and where my hero could meet with God I was certainly influenced by the low-tech approach of the inspiring 1976 BBC production of *I, Claudius,* and particularly by the sinister depiction of the Sibyl as a deathly Greek theatre mask levitating in the darkness of the cave.

I originally envisaged writing a short screenplay – beginning, middle, and end – with a notional idea that as an unfunded film project, using a minimal amateur cast and my own limited experience, it might take 5 or 6 months to make. I'm writing this in June 2016, some two-and-a-half years later. All going well *Axis Mundi*, although lacking a cast of thousands, will be able to proudly boast a '3 years in the making' tagline. Like most short independent films this is a passion project with very little in the way of budget. Despite this, I set out to make a cinematic piece. A film dealing with notions of godhead should be of epic proportions after all. A lot of time has been spent in developing the visual aesthetic with contemporary post-production techniques. Any amateur sleuth will note the use of green-screen technology as well as some basic visual effects. I have enjoyed learning about these processes and I've tried to ensure that the post-production design serves the story, as well as bringing added-value to the visual sense of the film. *Axis Mundi* has a dystopian sensibility. It also references ecclesiastical and iconic religious imagery.

Demarcus' journey is a dark, mystical – possibly a chemically induced – affair. We are unsure if he is journeying to a good or a bad place and the sound references this ambiguity. The *Axis Mundi* theme was created for the trailer and is directly influenced by sound artist Brian Eno with, I think, a little dash of Erik Satie. Another theme borrows from Miklós Rózsa, the man who scored *Ben Hur* (1960). This epic of all epic scores has a suitably biblical scale. When in doubt get the big Roman trumpets out.

The landscape shots within the film are very important, particularly in the latter part of the film where I had to create my undiscovered country. Everything was shot within a 30 mile radius of the Lyndhurst 102 Production Studios (otherwise known as our house in Newport-on-Tay). Little pockets of landscape around the east coast of Fife proved ideal for providing the otherworldly quality needed for, what I labelled, the 'Hinterland' section of the film. Perhaps the best way to describe the desired aesthetic is that I wanted something that was real, yet reminiscent of a 1960's *Star Trek* studio set. The location delivered admirably on aesthetic; we took a small stretch of coastline at Elie in the East Neuk of Fife and – with a little bit of post-production tinkering – turned the seaside idyll into a violent and menacing volcanic landscape.

One of my key aims from the beginning of this project was to create a well-written, engaging piece of work that would cost very little but, at the same time, stand up to scrutiny in terms of production values and visual punch. In the past,

film-making was very much the preserve of large well-funded studios and an elite group of highly-skilled artists and craftsmen. Recent technological advances, particularly concerning the transition from celluloid to digital film-making, have entirely changed the production landscape. When Orson Welles was invited to Hollywood by RKO to make his first movie – which eventually became *Citizen Kane* – he likened the experience to being given 'the biggest electric train set a boy ever had.' This is my 'digital train' set. Whether I successfully meet the intellectual and aesthetic goals that I've set for my own wee *Citizen Kane* remains to be seen. This will undoubtedly be debated over several pints of Guinness when I next return to Mulligan's.

Robert MacFarlane

Ghostline

"So the past makes its crazed
way into the future."

My neighbour's house is falling down. Its easterly extension has started to sag. A crack zigs down the brickwork from the guttering, then zags into the flowerbed and out of sight. Other houses nearby suffer similar problems. The fissure on one is so wide you can lay a finger in it. We shore up our properties with brackets and bolts, sink new foundations, glue glass slides across the cracks and wait for them to shatter. So the past makes its crazed way into the future.

For a long time, the cause of the subsidence was mysterious. Why did one house slump while its neighbour remained firm? Then a surveyor took a street-map of south Cambridge, and plotted the positions of the collapsing houses, marking each with a cross. The crosses fell into a line that ran straight south-east, then kinked ten degrees west, then ran straight again. He compared his marked street map with geological maps of the area, to see if there were a correlation between earth-type and subsidence. No correlation. He compared it with maps of gas mains, water pipes, sewage systems. No correlation. He compared it with land maps of the area dating from before the building of the first houses there. Snap.

During the summer of 1940, fears of a German invasion of Britain were at their height. The East Anglian coast was among the likeliest landing zones for any invasion force. The mudflats and saltmarshes of Essex, the shingle of Orford, the sands of Holkham, Southwold and Walberswick: such places, with their soft North Sea surf and their absence of cliffs, made ideal beachheads. East Anglia set about defending itself from attack:

something it had been doing, on and off, for over two thousand years. First, a coastal crust was established of low-tide landing spikes, barbed-wire aprons, minefields, trenches, and batteries. Thousands of anti-tank obstacles were cast in cement and dragged on to the beaches like outsize play-blocks – cones, cubes, cylinders, dragons' teeth. Inland, running parallel to the coast, was a series of stop-lines. In the event of the crust being breached, these were the lines to which defenders would successively fall back. The most important was the GHQ or General Headquarters Line, fortified by pillboxes and anti-tank trenches, which began in Somerset, ran along the south coast, hooked round Hellfire Corner, and then pushed up through East Anglia and as far north as Yorkshire.

If you look at a map of the East Anglian stretch of the GHQ Line, you will see that, about a mile south of Cambridge, the line splits into two, passes to either side of the city, before re-braiding about a mile to its north. In this way, Cambridge is left isolated within a ring-shaped island. This was because Cambridge had been designated a 'Defended Place': meaning that, in the case of invasion, it was expected to hold out independently. It was classified as a citadel that might slow the German assault, if the line itself could not be held.

A German military map of Cambridge from 1940 shows that plans for the taking of the city were far advanced. Crossroads are circled and pillboxes marked. It is now known that Hitler had already decided on Trinity College as his regional headquarters, and that Hermann Goering

– a connoisseur of Elizabethan architecture – intended to seize Burghley House near Stamford as his country pad. Preparations for the defence of Cambridge were assiduous, and somewhat hopeless. One Home Guardsman remembered that he and 'a Classics Professor' were given a single Stokes mortar, and 'told to stop the Third Panzer as it crossed the Mill Bridge'. Other defenders pored over Tom Wintringham's *New Ways of War*, a Penguin Special published in June 1940, which taught them how to simulate mines by placing upturned soup plates on the road (a halted tank became vulnerable to 'sticky bombs'), how to construct a home-made grenade using plumber's piping and pencils, and how to turn domestic houses into fortified strongholds.

Among the defensive works undertaken in Cambridge that busy summer was the excavation of an anti-tank trench. The trench, which formed part of the GHQ line, was nearly a mile long, cutting south-east across the city's flank. It was dug partly by reservists using mechanical excavators, and partly by volunteer civilians using spades. In profile, the trench was trapezoidal, with a berm on its eastern rim. It was around eighteen feet wide and eleven feet deep: big enough to swallow a Panzer.

The invasion never came, of course. Operation Sea Lion stalled. No landing craft beached on the Suffolk shingle or the Essex saltmarshes. No tanks rolled eastwards and inland. The Classics Professor stood down, the soup plates were scrubbed clean, and returned to the table. And shortly after Armistice, the spades and the diggers came out again and Cambridge's anti-tank trench was filled in.

Robert MacFarlane
Ghostline

"If you look at aerial photographs of fields to the south of Cambridge, you can still see the route of the trench. It's expressed in the growth of the crops – the wheat grows slightly less high where the trench used to run. When the trench leaves the fields and enters the city, it marks its route with a crack here, a slump there. Seventy years on from Armistice, the land here still carries memories of war."

But the earth that was used to infill the trench was insufficiently well tamped down. In the 1950s, Cambridge began to expand its limits, spreading its suburbia south. Houses were built across the line of the trench. The earth there wasn't able to give the foundations the firm context they required. Over the course of decades, the trench-earth settled, foundations shifted and grumbled, brickwork sagged, and cracks began to appear in those houses that straddled the line of the trench.

If you look at aerial photographs of fields to the south of Cambridge, you can still see the route of the trench. It's expressed in the growth of the crops – the wheat grows slightly less high where the trench used to run. When the trench leaves the fields and enters the city, it marks its route with a crack here, a slump there. Seventy years on from Armistice, the land here still carries memories of war.

East Anglia has always been front-line. It looks east, over the North Sea, towards old enemies: Germany, Holland, France, Denmark. For millennia, invaders have eyed up the Wash, the Blackwater, the Crouch – wide, soft-sided estuaries tonguing in to the centre of England.

There has been no successful invasion of the East Anglian coast since a Viking force won the Battle of Maldon in 991. But thousands of years of perceived threat have been enough to transform the region's appearance. The landscape has assumed a paranoid form. Defensive structures from over two thousand years litter the countryside. Earthworks, fortresses, watchtowers, castles, fox-holes, hangars, air fields, bunkers, sound-mirrors, listening posts, pillboxes, mortar pits, batteries, missile-silos.... How did Freud define paranoia? ' A disorder characterised by delusions of persecution, and often strenuously defended with apparent logic and reason.'

Among the earliest of East Anglia's defences were the Forts of the Saxon Shore, the chain of coastal strongholds established in the third-century AD by Carausius, a Belgic Gaul who became a commander in the Roman army, before rebelling and declaring himself independent Emperor of Britain. Following his death (assassination; poison; his trusted treasurer) the Carausian forts were occupied by the Romans, who in turn used them to defend the coast against Saxon raiders. After Carausius came era on era of defensive building. Orford Castle, constructed in 1165. The Martello Towers (red-bricked, thick-walled) built along the coast to repel a Napoleonic invasion. The First World War batteries, established to shoot down the Zeppelin bombers that came looming over the North Sea on calm nights. The Second World War radar masts at Bawdsey Manor in Suffolk – curious wooden structures more than eighty yards high that creaked in the wind. The sixty-seven new airfields established across East Anglia from 1939 onwards, out of which the Eighth Airfleet alone flew missions that used a billion gallons of fuel, dropped seven hundred and thirty-two thousand tons of bombs, and lost almost nine thousand aircraft and fifty

thousand men. The L-shaped blastwalls near Mepal, a village to the north of Cambridge, which mark the launch sites of the THOR intercontinental ballistic missiles from the early Cold War years. RAF Molesworth, where a fleet of Cruise missiles – snub-nosed, stubby-winged, and white as a Stormtrooper's body armour – were stored in silos.

Most of these structures are sinking back into the land, reclaimed by grass, moss, lichen. Swallows nest inside pillboxes. Peregrines breed on the Maunsell sea-forts off the Essex coast. Owls ghost at dusk from the battlements of the Martello Towers. They have become ruins: found sculptures, stumbled across on a walk or a bicycle-ride, or glimpsed from a train window. Anti-tank blocks stacked in a trackside wood, overgrown by ivy and bindweed, camouflaged with lurid lichens (lime, tangerine). Spigot mortar pedestals sitting, like curling stones, on the village green in Stowmarket. Mortar pits in Saffron Walden, and in Cley. Pillboxes built in the sea-wall on the Dengie Peninsula, or still guarding crossroads in North Norfolk.

Some of these structures have been abandoned. Others have been adapted: generations of Norfolk teenagers have been taken for driving practice on the county's disused airstrips. Almost all of these structures are crumbling, pried apart by rust, oxidisation, ivy. Pieces of them are pocketed by passers-by; cairns are made of the rubble. To dilapidate: [L *dilapidare*, f. di- + *lapis*, *lapid*-stone] 'to remove a stone or stones from'. Once you have begun to notice the militarisation of the East Anglian landscape, it can be hard to see

Robert MacFarlane

Ghostline

anything else. For this is a terrain more densely layered with martial pasts than any other area of Britain. In *The Rings of Saturn*, the German writer W.G. Sebald, who lived in Norwich for most of his life, describes a walking-tour through Suffolk. The deep saturation of that county by anticipated or actual violence is so affective and relentless that it brings Sebald's narrator to the point of nervous breakdown.

It is no surprise that this paranoid region should have inspired so many fantasias of attack, so many neurotic visions. The duel between the warship and the Martian Tripods that takes place in H.G. Wells' *War of the Worlds*, for instance, occurs just off the Essex coast. In 1903, Erskine Childers published T*he Riddle of the Sands*, his best-selling scare-novel about a German invasion centred on The Wash. Or one thinks – a different kind of narrative, this – of the big UFO conspiracies of the 1980s, when major landings were reputed to have occurred at Bentwaters and Rendlesham Forest, both in Suffolk. Then there is J.G. Ballard's 1967 story, 'Storm-Bird, Storm-Dreamer', which is set in an unspecified future on an unnamed estuarial Norfolk marshland. Its main character is a man called Crispin, who has taken charge of a wrecked boat, armed with anti-aircraft guns. His job is to shoot down the gigantic gulls, gannets, petrels, doves, and falcons that regularly attack the East Anglian coast in search of food – and which have reached their vast sizes due to excessive pesticide use.

Norfolk, Cambridgeshire, Suffolk, Essex: four front-line counties haunted by millennia of invasion dreams. What happens to the people of a region devoted to defence? What does such devotion do to the culture of an area, to its imagination?

One answer is that it breeds insularity. Resistance to any kind of incursion, a cultural defensiveness. This is, certainly, a common account of East Anglianism: as a region that is conservative, closed; as somewhere it takes a family four hundred years to qualify as local; somewhere that villages and peninsulas that secrete their own aspic or amber, suspend themselves in time. This is the kind of East Anglianism portrayed in Graham Swift's novel *Waterland*, where a shallow gene-pool and low social mobility have led to idiocy, madness and tragedy.

There is another, less cartoonish cultural consequence of East Anglia's defensive history. And this has to do with the nature or texture of truth. Rumour, hearsay, ambiguity – all thrive in East Anglia. So much secrecy has been required in this militarised landscape, so much disinformation perpetrated, that at times East Anglia seems to possess its own indigenous attitude to truth, as something provisional, or existing in a state of finely agitated uncertainty.

One thinks of the decoy airfields of the Second World War, with their dummy flarepaths, designed to draw the ordnance of German bombers. Or of the false fireboxes – sparks and flames in the darkness – lit during air-raids over Norfolk to simulate marshalling yards. Or of the secret

network of fox-holes and bunkers, scattered through the woods and fields of the region, to which the 'Stay-Behinds' (the Home Guards trained to form a partisan resistance in case of occupation) were to fall back. Similar examples of dissembling and deceit could be drawn from every defensive era of East Anglia's history. Centuries of concealment have rendered certain types of truth – cartographical, geographical – friable, fissile.

This quality to knowledge is in keeping with the region's landscape. For the geological equivalents of rumour and speculation are sand and shingle. Nothing stays still on this region's long coastline. Spits and bars are born by one storm and abolished by the next. Maps are forever having to be redrawn. The East Anglian littoral does not possess the igneous reliability of the northern and western rims of Britain. The edgelands here are constantly ceding to the sea, or weaving with it. There is an eeriness to them that is born of their perpetual motion, and the dialogue between solid and liquid. It can often be hard to say quite where the land begins and the sea ends. East Anglia has less a coastline than a ghostline.

Nowhere is this reciprocal quality of truth and of land more apparent than on Orford Ness: the vast shingle spit – twelve miles long and up to two miles wide – that lies off the coast of Suffolk, and which has for decades been the site of high-secrecy military work. A psycho-geographer's dowsing rod, passed over a map of East Anglia, would leap from the hand as it neared Orford.

Robert MacFarlane
Ghostline

"Aerial images of Blakeney show it to possess the complex beauty of a neuron: the long stem of the spit, and to its leeward a marshland that floods and emerges with every tide – a continually self-revising labyrinth of channel and scarp."

The Ness is the largest and strangest of the series of vast shingle peninsulas that jut from the coastlines of Norfolk, Suffolk, Essex and Kent. To its north are Scolt Head and Blakeney Point, and to its south is Dungeness, the fulcrum on which the North Sea pivots into the English Channel. These spits are created by the action of tides, currents and seasonal storms. Like sand dunes, they are in continual slow migration, forming and reforming their shape as they shift. In their movement, they are as close to organism as anything only mineral can be. They organise themselves in designs so large that they are best witnessed from the vantage of a falcon or an airman. At Dungeness, the shingle is arranged into giant floreate blooms. Orford forms itself in long parallel ridges, each of which marks a time when a storm has cast up thousands of tonnes of gravel along the shore, and fattened the spit. These ridges are the stone equivalents of growth-rings in a tree trunk. Aerial images of Blakeney show it to possess the complex beauty of a neuron: the long stem of the spit, and to its leeward a marshland that floods and emerges with every tide – a continually self-revising labyrinth of channel and scarp.

The Ness has no permanent population, and for its thousands of grey acres, the only moving things are hares, hawks, and the sea-wind. It is a desert, really, a desert of shingle. For eighty years, it was owned by the Ministry of Defence, which prized its natural security cordon, as well as its uniformity and expanse.

So it was that like other, larger deserts – the Great Victoria in Australia, the Kizil Kum in Kazakhstan, the Mojave Desert in America – the Ness became a site for military testing. Bomb ballistics and weaponry experiments were conducted on the Ness during the First and Second World Wars, and in the 1960s, nuclear detonation devices were trialled – shock-tested, heat-tested, vibration -tested – in specially built concrete structures now known as The Pagodas.

All across the Ness, enigmatic military structures still protrude from the shingle – pre-fabricated barracks, listening stations, beacons, watch-towers, bunkers, blast-chambers. Unexploded ordnance lies around, concealed in the shingle. It is forbidden to step off certain cleared pathways, which have been made safe and are marked out with a rust-red dye and blood-red arrows. By the sides of the pathways lie military debris: twisted sprays of tank tracking, a shattered concrete block, and an exploded boiler, whose inch-thick iron casing has flared into bright rusted thick petals. Warnings not to stray, to keep to the line.

On a May day of mixed weathers, I travelled out to see the Ness. With me were my friends Leo Mellor, a poet and military historian, and Jules Pretty, an environmental scientist and writer: good companions for a strange place. The Ness is now owned by the National Trust, and one of the Trust's wardens, Grant, had agreed to boat us over, and escort us round the site.

We met Grant on the Orford quay. Dinghy lanyards clacked and gossiped. Swifts cross-bowed through the air above us. Grant was wearing a work-stained green National Trust sweatshirt. His beard was big enough to qualify as an

ecosystem. He had been working on the Ness since the handover from the MoD, for nearly fifteen years, he told us. And this meant that he knew everything there was to know about the Ness, which included knowing that knowing everything wasn't possible. We chugged in a converted trawler across the tidal reach of the River Ore, towards the Ness. Grant steered with a loose hand on the tiller. 'The first rule of Orford Ness,' he said, 'is that you don't believe anything anyone tells you'. We waited. 'And the second rule is that you don't believe anything you say yourself'.

He nodded back towards the wooded shore from which we had just pulled away. 'Same goes for the mainland round here. The woods are filled with inexplicable stuff.'

Once on the Ness itself, we climbed into a white Landrover, and Grant set off, jolting over the pitted tarmac. First we traversed marshland sluiced by a series of dykes and swatchways. Then we rattled over a bridge – curlew probing the mud beneath – and onto the shingle of the Ness proper. Long open sightlines. The light radiating white off the stones, giving the feel of a desert's metallic brightness. Shelducks – snooker-player smart in green and black – rising in pairs, threes, as we drove past, and drifting off to settle at a distance.

Small discrete weather systems – squalls, sun-slants – moved in and over us, out towards the sea, smacking rain and light down on to the vehicle's windscreen. We passed blast holes in the shingle: like ant-lion pits, but up to fifteen yards wide. They had been made, Grant told us, anything up

Robert MacFarlane

Ghostline

"All around the laboratory, hundreds of red valerian flowers swung and bobbed in the wind, self-seeded along the edges of concrete, and in shingle niches. 'Invader species', Grant said. 'Plenty of those here."

to ninety years previously. But the shingle had held the impression of the blasts with integrity: it looked as though the bombs had fallen a week ago, not almost a century. 'There's so much ordnance still lying around.' Grant said. 'We usually have the Bomb Disposal boys over here, maybe twenty times a year. Somewhere out there are two Grandslams. Conventional bombs don't come much bigger than that.'

'Once, in the early years, we found a big old drainpipe. We got the JCB over to dig it out. But when we'd got it in the shovel, we found it wasn't a drainpipe. No, it was an anti-aircraft fragmentation missile, proximity-trigged, with a napalm core. Live. Nothing's ever what it looks like out here.'

We drove east, then south, towards the pagodas. Grant pulled up next to one of them. 'Lab Four', he said. We got out. All around the laboratory, hundreds of red valerian flowers swung and bobbed in the wind, self-seeded along the edges of concrete, and in shingle niches. 'Invader species', Grant said. 'Plenty of those here. We've dug out a potato plant, daffodils. As for the foxes…They swim over from the mainland, coming after the rabbits and hares. And we shoot them.'

Through chain-link gates, I could see the interior of the laboratory: a sunken space, thirty feet deep and twenty across, its floor filled with shards of glass, concrete, rusted iron. Due east, a big slow moving rainstorm was visible. Black cumulonimbus, thousands of feet high, with dark tendrils of rain moving slowly beneath it – a jellyfish storm.

'Look north from here,' said Grant, 'and you'll see no more land for a thousand miles. When you do next make landfall, it'll be in the Arctic Circle. So when the northerlies blow, it gets properly cold. A special-issue great coat was given to those who worked on Orford. And a rum ration. Do you know where the only other place you got a rum ration was? Christmas Island.' Grant sounded proud of this, as though he were the inheritor of the same austerity culture.

He told us about the work that had gone on in the Lab. It was down there that the testing of the first-generation nuclear warheads had taken place during the 1950s. Fat, gleaming bath-toy missiles with their stubby wings and their rainbow-coded nursery names: Blue Danube, Yellow Sun, Orange Herald. He said that he couldn't be quite sure about the nature of the work – whether there had ever actually been a primed physics package in this laboratory, or even anywhere on the Ness.

'This is the thing,' said Grant, 'about the Ness. The economy of disinformation and misinformation. Almost everything I've ever been told about this place has subsequently proved to be untrue, or at least unreliable.'

The pagoda was disintegrating. Rusted girders showed through part-dissolved concrete. The guttering bled dark streaks down the cement. Grass grew opportunistically in crannies. When Grant wasn't looking, I stooped and palmed up an arrowhead-shaped fragment of rusted iron. 'The management policy of a place like this', said Grant, 'is known as Controlled Ruination.

Which basically means we let things fall apart in their own time. No point doing otherwise. Because the buildings all have inherent concrete cancer. The salt – the salt that was mixed into the concrete to stop it freezing. Now it's causing oxidation, expansion, cracking. Everything's slowly dilapidating.' I felt less guilty about having taken the fragment.

Grant boated us back across the Ore. As we drove out of Orford, Jules put on Johnny Cash's 'The Wanderer'. 'I went out walking / Under an atomic sky….'. I turned my found piece of Ness iron in my hands. It was roughly wedge-shaped, three inches long, two wide, and half an inch deep. It had been eroded by salt and wind into a state of gorgeously elaborate ruination, layered, stepped and stratified: the relief map of terraced hill country, or a shore-line eaten away in increments by the sea.

The oldest invasion faced by East Anglia is not human in nature, but marine. The North Sea is the greatest and least repudiable of all East Anglia's aggressors. The threat of inundation haunts both the region's landscape and its imagination. Large areas of Norfolk and Essex are reclaimed land, stolen back from the sea by an ingenious system of sea walls, pumps, dykes, and fleams. This is provisional terrain, borrowed territory, ghosted by water.

At unpredictable moments, the sea reasserts itself in great diluvial acts. The disastrous tide of

Robert MacFarlane

Ghostline

"Historical events such as these have become prophetic. They provide us with images not only of the East Anglian past, but also of the region's likely near-future."

Martinmas 1099, recorded in the Anglo-Saxon Chronicle: 'This year also, on the festival of St. Martin, the sea-flood sprung up to such a height, and did so much harm, as no man remembered that it ever did before. And this was the first day of the new moon.' Or the storm-surged spring tide of January 31st 1953 that killed hundreds across the region, and submerged Essex as far inland as Tillingham.

Historical events such as these have become prophetic. They provide us with images not only of the East Anglian past, but also of the region's likely near-future. For as global warming results in heightened sea-levels, the soft, low coasts of Norfolk, Suffolk and Essex will be among those that suffer first – and most. Hypothetical dissolve-maps, which show in detail the territorial consequences of different sea-level rises, reveal a future East Anglia that is laced through again with water. A region reduced – in the most severe scenarios – to little more than a series of islands joined by causeways.

At present, nowhere is more front-line in the defensive war against the sea than the Easton Bavents: the mile-long stretch of coastline and cliff immediately north of Southwold. The Bavents land is owned by a man called Peter Boggis. Jules knew Boggis well, and suggested that we meet him. So we trundled out of Southwold and uphill, towards the ramshackle buildings of the Bavents. Ragged Steptoe-and-son style farmland. A flock of Manx rams grazing and lazing behind a barbed-wire fence, horns like ammonites. Skylarks ticker-taping their song down from fifty feet up.

Jules pulled up outside the tangle of houses and barns, the nearest of them only thirty yards from the cliff edge. Between that house and the cliff was a vast pile of masonry rubble, on which sat a crook-armed JCB. Swallows sat in twos and threes on the telephone wires, their tails sharp as dividers. And a steady stream of sand martens slipped through the air to their nest-holes in the sandy cliffs.

Peter came out to meet us. Seventy, perhaps, with a thick-weave jumper and cord trousers shiny from use. Working clothes, decades old. He had a slight limp, and carried a shepherd's crook to help him walk. We stood together on the crumbling cliff edge, and Peter began to speak. He had lived on The Bavents land almost all his life, he said. During the war, his family refused to evacuate him along with the other children of Southwold, and so he had stayed on while the land was militarised around him. 'There was almost nothing to eat,' he said, 'so we lived wild. Caught fish, rabbits, picked sea-kale, took water-hen's eggs from the marshes.'

'Two 6-inch gun emplacements were established in the woods just up there', he said, jabbing northwards with his crook. 'Anti-tank trenches were dug just inland of our property. A battalion of men moved in to the Bavents. They became my friends; there was nobody of my age left around here.'

'What you must understand', he said then, 'is that we've lost three hundred yards of land since the end of the war.' Using the tip of his crook,

he scratched a map in the mud. Two lines, one showing the present-day coastline. The other, the ghostline, bowing far outwards, showing the littoral of 1945. He scribbled in the section between the two lines. 'This is what the sea has won', he said. Then he pointed out to sea. 'See that boil of white water?' A steady gout of turbulence was just visible, perhaps fifty yards out. 'That is the site of a Cold War listening tower,' Peter said. 'Built in 1962 as part of the radar cover, sixty metres back from the cliff-edge. Now look where it is.'

Peter's sight did not stop at the surface of the sea. He looked through it, to the submerged landscape he had once known. 'Out there are hundreds of tank-blocks, three-foot cubes. We used them as stepping-stones to get through the minefield and down into town.' 'There' – a seawards sweep of the crook – 'are the steel spikes which were set at the low-water mark. 'There' – a jab – 'is the anti-tank scaffolding.'

Three hundred yards of lost land. And now Peter's house was close to joining the other submarine relics. Ten years ago, he said, English Nature, the agency charged with sea defence, had acceded to a policy of 'managed retreat'. 'Abandonment is what that means'.

So Peter began to mount his own defence. He charged builders in the region a small fee to dump their building rubble off the edge of his cliffs. The builders were glad to have such a cheap method of disposal. Soon, hundreds of lorries from across the region were thundering up to the Easton Bavents.

Robert MacFarlane

Ghostline

'Twelve thousand lorry-loads to date', said Peter proudly. 'Around eighteen tons of rubble each lorry. The most I brought through the town in one day was one hundred and twenty-five vehicles.'

His plan was that the rubble should permanently shore up the cliffs. In front of the rubble he would keep tipping a sacrificial frontage of gravel and bricks: clean and friable material, which would 'give the sea something to chew on'. So he had fought, day by day, year by year, to defend his diminishing land from the advancing sea. An East Anglian Canute. The environmental agencies had done their best to prevent his dumping, and he had become disliked by many of the Southwoldians, for spoiling the look of the beach.

During the winter of 2006–07, he has suffered a severe setback. In early December, the wind had swung round to a northerly, and stuck there for weeks. Within two days, the beach level had dropped by three metres. Storm waves coming across the Bavents bay struck the rubble blockade directly. Thirty metres of land were bitten back by the sea in the four weeks that followed: ten times the total average annual erosion rate.

'In 1640', Peter said, looking far out to sea, 'the land ran out here for a further three-and-a-half kilometres. It was protected by peat beds to north and south, born when this region was near-tropical forest. But later in the seventeenth century, once the firewood had all been used up, people started to look elsewhere for fuel. The maltings industry was booming at that time, and they needed fuel for the drying. So of course they started to use the peat.

They ran big barges on to the peat beds, waited for low tide, dug the peat on to the barges, then let high tide float the boats off. Back on land, they then dried the peat and burnt it.'

'In this way', he said, 'they destroyed the best natural sea defence East Anglia ever had'.

Late that afternoon, to end the day, Jules, Leo and I drove down to Shingle Street. Shingle Street is a remote coastal village, just south of Orford Ness, reachable along a series of narrowing roads. Originally a fishing village, it is little more than a handful of pretty whitewashed houses in a seawards-facing line. Three Martello Towers guard the estuary immediately to the village's south. And of course there is shingle. Acres of it. A shifting shingle shore over four miles long and up to three-hundred-yards deep.

On the way there, we listened to Johnny Cash's 'I Walk The Line'. We parked at the road's end, and crunched over the shingle towards the sea. The water here was in a testy, tidal mood. A fierce tiderip was running, tilting the marker buoys northwards. The wind was stronger, and the light less bright than on the Ness.

Right against the waterline, the waves had thrown up a ten-foot-high sloped rampart of wet shingle. We scrambled down it, the stones hissing and slithering under our feet, and then we walked along the tide line, picking up pieces of wood, comparing flints. The shingle rampart locked off the rest of the world. There was only the steep wet gravel to our west, and the sea to our east, brown and frightening. Fast, fat, stone-heavy waves plunged aggressively, and the big wind filled the air with cold spray. I could hear only the detonations of the waves, gravel spattering like bullets, and the wind's steady roar. It was not hard to see how this distant front-line space had drawn and generated so many rumours.

After a few hundred yards, we decided to turn back. So we climbed straight back up the rampart, intending to cut diagonally across the shingle and back to the car.

Then there was the start of the line. It was made of rock whelks, thousands upon thousands of them, their shells bleached bright white, laid side by side. Fifty or so shells to the yard, and the line ran for hundreds of yards: meandering away from us, dipping and rising over the shingle dunes, inland and out of sight. It began at no particular point – simply emerged, like a river surfacing after miles underground. Where it met a clump of sea cabbage or sea kale, it split into two, passed to either side of the clump, then re-braided again.

Who had made it? And why? But neither question, I realised, was of interest or value. The line had been made, and was beautiful, and its gratuity was its point. It was innocent, childish and freely given. It was also, I realised, the only line we had encountered that day which ran inland. Defensive lines – disputed, purposeful – hem the coast: they run parallel to the littoral. This line, however, meandered at a rough perpendicular to the coast, and in this respect its course was most like a river.

So we followed the shell-river inland, walking back towards the sun, holding the line. The sea out there to the east, where it would always be, with the weather, waiting.

Poetry

Peter Davidson

Four Variations on Exile and Return

"Westward over the tree tops the red glow lights us lovingly; eastward under the branches of each green valley, the reeds whisper in the twilight. Content drops from heaven, peace breathes from the forest."

Evening Music

O that I were beyond the waves at the frontiers of evening. Today flows to yesterday, gone on the waters of time.

You are peace at nightfall, you are gentleness and rest, you are longing and all that quietens longing to stillness. I offer my eyes and heart as your home; in sorrow or joy, my heart and eyes. Come to me through the dim rooms, the silent rooms, the enfilade of evening. Softly close the door behind you. Still all pain, fill my heart, draw forth delight. Brow pale as hawthorn over still green water. Fill my soul with the evenings of your eyes. O eyes the green reflection of summer twilight under the boughs. Of hawthorn hedges and far summer rain. So deep into the green, the rainfall, the dimming day. O rest and gentleness at last.

O that I were beyond the waves at the frontiers of evening. Today flows to yesterday, gone on the waters of time. O evening star, O star of the Queen of Love.

On the mirror of the waters, the swan-boat glides, our souls glide forth on those same streams. Dropping from the heavens to the waters, the lights of evening glimmer round the boat.

Westward over the tree tops the red glow lights us lovingly; eastward under the branches of each green valley, the reeds whisper in the twilight. Content drops from heaven, peace breathes from the forest. Time glides with dew wet wings, away across the distant waters. Tomorrows will pass on glimmering wings, today flows to yesterday, gone on the waters of time. And so it glides and vanishes and flows, until I rise on westering wing away from time and all its alterations. O evening star. O star of the Queen of Love. O rest and gentleness at last.

Today flows to yesterday, gone on the waters of time, gone beyond the waves, far at the frontiers of evening.

Rain and the early dark.

Onslaught of rain with the bitter wind behind it. Unremitting, day-long, obliterating, splintering rain, hammering an East Anglian coastal town. Rain scouring and driving down cobbled streets.

There is a fine Georgian House at the top of the town: rubbed brick and Portland stone, white-painted glazing-bars in long windows, a wrought-iron arch with a lantern over the gate. There is a walled garden on the cliff-top behind, facing the sea mist and the invasion of the rain. The best bedroom of the house is loud with the sound of the rain and dim with filtered light from mist and dark sky, dimmed further by heavy green curtains. There is a painted landscape of cornfields and old trees let into the panelling above the fireplace.

In the tall mahogany bed with its looped-up hangings, a young patrician drowses in his parents' sheets. It is the day after his widowed mother's funeral, he half-awakens alone in a house which is newly his. Rain at the windows, storm in the chimney. He wakens fully for a moment, with a sense that he must meet someone urgently that day. But he dozes again, remembering that it is a Saturday and that the appointment with the solicitor is on Monday morning before he goes back to London. He stretches legs and back between warm sheets, half thinking that he should get up, go for a walk or run. He hears the rain and drowses again, thinking or dreaming of the path from the back gate of the garden and his boat moored below the cliffs. He stretches and relaxes, aware of his own strength and nakedness, as he falls asleep ever deeper under the rain.

Late in the afternoon he raids what was his boyhood room, grim in the light of one bare bulb, and half-dresses in his school rugby shirt and tracksuit trousers. He slips boat shoes onto cold feet and slouches downstairs to eat expensive left-overs from the fridge. At four o'clock twilight, the wind dies: the last grey light from the seaward windows falls into the panelled rooms. He roams through the darkening house and looks for a moment out over the sea. In the town, the yellow streetlights are coming on. The walled garden and the waters beyond are consumed by rain and the early dark.

On a boat out to sea in the twilight and misty rain, a woman comes out onto the deck as the wind dies. She looks at the humped outline of the town, the lightless manor on the cliffs. She looks to landward, at the rain marbling the long reflections of the harbour-lights. The bulkhead light gleams in the smallest drops of water in her hair. She stares at the land until the dark falls – cobalt, blue-green, black – then orders her boat to sail out, northwards and away through the sodden air.

Peter Davidson

Four Variations on Exile and Return

"To live in a silent house beside water, withdrawn into the steep valley, going into the coastal towns only under cover of autumn or winter nightfall, to the red stone inland villages only under the protection of the summer dawn."

The young man goes back to bed not long after nightfall. Later, a voice speaks to him out of the empty house: *had you gone to her, your son might, in years to come, have made things less grievous than now they will be.*

The Lost Thing Found

Returning on a gentle sea through unshadowed night, landing on the shingle beach with the first light, returning in fear and discretion. Returning in secret, hoping for nothing more than to live privately and unobserved, in a landscape shaped by discretions and evasions. To live in a silent house beside water, withdrawn into the steep valley, going into the coastal towns only under cover of autumn or winter nightfall, to the red stone inland villages only under the protection of the summer dawn.

To go forth alone on minor roads to read the traces deep in the landscape – the ruined tower in the hanging wood by the narrows of the river – shafts of pale sun, nettles, flowering wild cherries. The road leading on through a farmyard before coming up out of the trees onto the bare slopes of the hill. The humped stone bridge far from any road, crossing the small water in the plantations around the remote house in the snowiest valley. The keystone broken, the stones of the parapets falling one by one into the pool of brown water below. So many years passed and the builders gone so long.

The farmhouse far above the treeline, with the snow-scars on the slopes above, one rowan clinging for shelter to the gable wall. Awaiting a day of farthest, upland pastoral at high summer, when its flowers and leaves together would cast still shadows through one windless day. The prodigality of wild raspberries growing on the stones of the ruined steading at the foot of the sheer hill with the ramparts on its summit.

Forests of birch and Scots pine, ferny underwoods. False chanterelles and fallen birch leaves. October wind from the east, turning to cold and the winter. Sunlight uncertain and low between the trunks of the trees, falling on birch bark and colouring it dark yellow. Moss and pine needles over the paths. Sunlight faded, the sky yellowing and dimming with rain coming over. Wind more insistently cold. Turning for home. Murmuring and whirring in the distance, louder and higher, gathering intensity. Coming to the edge of the trees the grey sky momentarily full of migrating geese flying low, circling, settling out of sight.

Granite soldier at the church gate, guard us at the fall of day. Crow Stone on the bare hill, watch us through the dark of the year. Carved pillar of old battles, look out over the sea to the north.

Stone piles, once the wall of the policies, rise from the shingle of the foreshore; gate piers, canted and rusticated, with the end-rig of the sea-field ploughed hard against them. On either side of the long-burned avenue, red earth, and the larks rising into freezing morning air. Within, midwinter brilliance reflecting up from the marble floor long broken to the great painted ceiling, long shreds and coloured dust: the winter Persephone returned, the lost thing found.

The Boy from the North

A jumbled farmers' market on a vacant lot in the city, a mild, dark day just before Christmas – one stall selling only smoked fish and white farmhouse cheese. The stall keeper a tall fair boy in his early twenties – beautifully polite, but shy in trying to sell to strangers. I bought some herring and farmer's wife's white cheese, pleased to see his stock almost sold. His courtesy, accent and voice, and especially the way he could not let anyone pass without a greeting in that crowded place – all spoke of a village on the high headland overlooking the Pentland Firth, of the rough grey sea, the wind-formed trees. His high colour and tow fair hair, his quietly measured speech, all spoke of the nearness of Orkney and the islands beyond. Soon he would pack up, with darkness already falling on the city, and drive for hours on end through Inverness, over the Kessock Bridge, past Tain and the slopes behind Helmsdale. Far into the winter night, he would stop the van at last and step out into cold air and the insistence of the sea. Because of all these things, I wept unseen in the dark lane behind the square, not only because I knew myself, for that moment, his countryman and in exile from a storm-riven, decent land beyond the mountains, which comes and goes and is not always there.

Art

Merran Gunn

Lullaby

This installation, *Lullaby* (2016), is a continuation of an earlier piece I made for events in Edinburgh and Dundee, *The Lament Room*. That work was based on the death scene of John Sutherland, a piper who lived in 'The Grey House', Sutherland's family home, from the novel *The Big Music* by Kirsty Gunn. That installation explored the unravelling of the mind at the end of life and the solitary act of death, shown as a single bed in the downstairs box room of 'The Grey House', where the Highland piper lies dying surrounded by memory and snatches of music.

In *Lullaby*, I am working again with *The Big Music*, and exploring, in the context of *The Voyage Out*, the idea of 'being', of life itself, as not only containing lament and final voyage, but also that first voyage made from birth, from which all of us once started out.

Kirsty and I had the idea for *Lullaby* of using imagery of the beginning of life from within that same Highland family, from that same house, maybe even inside that same single room in which the old man dies. The cradle rocks gently to the humming of the mother's lullaby, and the gentle sounds of domestic life are heard in the background.

The installation uses the setting of the wooden cabins of the *Discovery* ship, moored at Dundee, to mimic the little room in The Grey House, with its centuries of protective family history and journeys. The wheels of the pram and the spinning wheel throw moving shadows across the old wooden floor, like the wheels of life itself. Music gently weaves through the young infant's mind, as it will continue to do through his long life.

The music composed for the installation uses the lyrics of the lullaby by Helen Mackay, also from *The Big Music*. I based this lullaby on the pio-baireachd *Lament for Himself*, that was composed from a fragment of the original composition by John Sutherland in *The Big Music*. I have added a Gaelic chorus to the lullaby which translates as 'You, yourself took her out into the wilderness.'

In the small room, a basket waits,
A basket empty for no baby is there.
The mother's gone, left the room for a moment
– and in that moment he's mounted the stair.

(chorus)
You took her away,
Young Katherine Anna,
Carried her off, tall Helen's child.
You took her away a baby sleeping
In your old arms, took her into the wild.

(second verse)
An old man taken the baby away.
He's snatched her up in his arms for to see.
Her life in his to stay his dying
but the child's not his, her mother is me.

(chorus)
You took her away,
Young Katherine Anna,
Carried her off, tall Helen's child.
You took her away, a baby sleeping
In your old arms took her into the wild.[1]

Dh'fhaibh thu leatha dan fhàsach

Manas Ray

Out of Silence

"Even then I did not know who exactly she was. I knew and also did not know. Information came in bits and pieces as I grew up. Her eerie resemblance to my mother bothered me."

One day, without notice, Pritikana came. We, brothers and sisters, did not know about her presence till she turned up that day along with her husband and their three-year old daughter. They started visiting us fairly regularly – initially once in every two weeks, then every week and more. The man was dark, very dark, had a chiseled nose and broad eyes. He was very lively. I remember him singing at times, sitting on the steps that led to the verandah – loud, unhesitant, full-throated, direct from the heart. The woman bore an eerie resemblance to my mother – the same height, the same face, the same complexion, the same voice, the same way of talking. She was, as if, what my mother must have been some twenty years back.

The child was about five years younger than me and, like any other child, soon became part of the family through her cries, tantrums and wonders. They all did, there was no way they couldn't: the man through his uninhibited manners and direct way of talking, a loud and clear voice, and she, my mother-surrogate, through her quick grasp of the family's folk history: the stock of gossip, the stories that circulated, the jokes, the memorable happenings of the past. She was affectionate and loving towards us, me and my siblings, and showed an ardent, even if ruffled, admiration and love for my parents.

Even then I did not know who exactly she was. I knew and also did not know. Information came in bits and pieces as I grew up. Her eerie resemblance to my mother bothered me. She became part of my childhood mystery, my sense of the unknown, and unknowingly, clouded with a moral ambiguity

I could not locate. Strangely enough, their presence brought a sense of jubilation too. I started hiding in that jubilation, always looking for something else than what was present, always uncertain, always cheerful.

The neighbourhood's reaction was complex. The happenings in our family were too mammoth for gossip but also the source of infinite curiosity. If I ever drifted in course of play to someone's courtyard and found myself in the midst of the afternoon chatter of women, maybe the too curious among them would ask me about the new family who visited us so often, mentioning Pritikana, her husband Sunil, and the child Tukun by their names. The gesture was to demonstrate familiarity and perhaps a restrained acceptance. The touch of extra affection was clear. It was part of good manners for the neighbourhood not to discuss the visitors in our presence, as if their very mentioning threatened to crumble the nascent social order and solidarity on which the riot-ridden refugee colony's existence depended. But curiosity remained. Was detachment in-built into the patterns of involvement of these mostly rural people from East Bengal thrown into the social turmoil of post-Partition Calcutta? Or, could it be that detachment and involvement depended on the position of the sun? The faces in the fading light, especially the older faces, looked distinctly detached, released as if for good from the claims of the everyday. The stories they recounted of a land now past became murmurs, barely audible, sighs. For the close relatives, who half knew about what had happened to my mother a long time ago, her arrival was a past calamity brought back to the present and quite unnecessarily. But in that way everyone was related to Priti just as we were – she was a niece, a cousin, a grand daughter and hence an object of affection.

My sister's sudden arrival in the family was also the cause for another kind of reshuffling. Anjali, the sister everybody knew as the eldest, was no more the eldest. Anjali was the center that held the family together, the fountain of love and affection. She was also the first among the siblings to realize who Priti actually was – my parents' first child and born before they were wed. She never told us then.

What seemed one explanation, one answer, never remained one. In order for any answer to be an answer, it had to return to that elusive point of origin, seek sanction from a past veiled from public eye but immensely real, and be relayed back from there through the intervening years right up to the present. The trail takes me back to my father's involvement in the independence movement, his early years in the terrorist outfit, Yugantar Party, his later conversion to Gandhism, his stints in the British prisons. Were they not actually married before Priti was born? Priti's foster mother, an ex-terrorist. Priti's ultra-modern, urbane but lonely upbringing in Calcutta – she played the *piano* for a refugee boy on the outskirts of Calcutta, the ultimate sign of Europe. What happened when my parents returned to Dhaka, leaving Priti to the care of her foster mother? Under what circumstances did they get married, formally and perhaps for the second time? Was it the Partition that made the re-union possible? Was it the Partition and its impact on moral codes that made it possible for

Manas Ray
Out of Silence

our neighbours to accept the happenings of our family silently? It all seemed like a kaleidoscope that gave a different picture with every turn.

As things started settling down, there was another turn of events, and in a way more traumatic than the first. Towards the mid-60s, and for a long while, my father's salary from the school became irregular. The family gained some notoriety from a photograph that appeared in the newspaper, showing my father and his colleagues on hunger strike next to the locked gate of the school. Anjali had completed her BA degree by then and, as one more enactment of the much-repeated refugee allegory, she took up a job as a junior stenographer in a government office. Marriage proposals were put on the backburner; her job came handy in stabilizing the listing boat that was our family. On the day she joined work, Anjali – like many other womenfolk in our locality – in starched and pressed printed saris, purse strapped on her shoulder was about to set off. Mother paused for a moment – blessed her thrice and went through the gesture of mock spitting once on her forehead, a ritual to ward off evil, reserved for special occasions. Father accompanied my sister to her office, a long red colonial building, number 3 Government Place in the city centre.

It turns out Anjali has been getting late coming back from the office every day . Quite often it is fairly late and past bedtime. The home gets restless waiting for her to return through the burnt brick-chip-laid lane. The moment I hear her heels clack-clacking on the red cemented verandah, I turn the other way round in my bed and close my

eyes. In the mornings when I wake up I find her doing the beds, humming absentmindedly, her face suffused with a hint of smile and eyes lit up with love.

It was eventually revealed that she was having an affair with Sunil, the husband of my eldest sister, Priti. My mother looked helpless in her agony. "While you all along have chosen your sarees, your ornaments" she said to her. "Now please let me choose the man for you". She looked helpless in her agony. I saw her sob in quiet corners of the house. Tears rolled Anjali's cheeks too, but she grew more resolute in her love. Finally my parents agreed to their marriage. By then I was 15, about to leave school.

My family's claim to ordinariness must have been enormous, for despite everything, it seemed so utterly ordinary, so reassuring, so normal, just like any other family. And this worried me, even annoyed me perhaps. I watched carefully the movement of the ants: in one row, each busy, each carrying something white in its mouth, the straggler falling behind, the dead one carried by others, a long procession of activities, a long chain of regularities. I watched the butterflies as they swung on our karamcha tree in one corner of our courtyard, the multiple, intricate patterns of their wings. I watched our betel nut tree, its soft, quiet, green pulp would remind me of Madhusree long after I left St Mary's. The red snake. I knew its movements from the rustle of dry leaves lying behind my room, watched it raise its hood, gently swing in the autumn breeze and go back to hiding again. The red snake would at times return at night, track lazily towards the pond, the weight of moonlight, blue like a grasshopper's body, on its back. At football, I waited eagerly for the ball to travel all the way to the goal, wrap itself mercilessly in the nets, and for the waves it caused. Everywhere, in whatever I saw, I discovered a network of deception. And love; its ordinariness and regularity made me feel impatient.

I found in Calcutta's Maoist politics, by then waning, the expression of my adolescence, and a good place to be. It introduced me to a new world of narrow lanes, meetings in dark, damp chambers, whispers, new words, new mappings, new kinds of excitement, a new sense of importance. I wasn't convinced by what they called their 'theory', their programmes, charts, and hopes. But I liked the way the raw betel nut smell of my adolescence mingled with that of hand-made grenades to create strange shapes in my dreams; I liked the way Swadhinda, the one who preached, and Bhakat Bhai, the local rice-mill owner whom we targeted for 'action', met as pre-historic beings in the wrinkled womb of darkness as I slept. For once, the circle of deceit was not exactly ordinary. But I wanted a quick passage, aiming always for the interrogation cell at Lord Sinha Road, head-quarters of the detective department of Calcutta Police. There, sitting next to a spotless, guiltless table, with a bright lamp as the unusually bright solitary witness that would at times be turned on my face, I would get ready for the encounter, challenging the prospect of torture that loomed large, all the time thinking of the willowy ripples of the pond, the red snake, a particular scrawny bird that sat in the path of the snake, and what

I took to be its faded wish. I played the game of deception well, as I knew I would. I felt vulnerable but was always released in a matter of days.

My father died. At 23, I thought I stood exposed. The city would take its revenge on me. I would be lynched. Half way through the month, I stopped going to the advertising agency where I worked and one day headed towards Howrah Station, making my way to an unreserved compartment of a Delhi-bound train. As I squeezed into the crowd, the smell of *khaini* comforting, the train started slowly moving. I could make out I was hiding again.

All that was once unspeakable I see is now a matter of writing.

Jeremy Poynting

'But England... What do you want with England?'

Almost thirty years ago, at the 1987 International Bookfair of Radical Black and Third World Books, my friend Jan Shinebourne, one of the first writers Peepal Tree published, reported a conversation she'd had with Linton Kwesi Johnson where he'd asked her who was the 'quiet Englishman" he'd seen her talking to. The phrase has stuck with me. At one level, I readily acknowledged both its elements, and still do, though these days I find I have an alarming amount to say; at another level the tag of *Englishman* was a reminder that whilst this was not how I went about describing myself, it was how I was seen.

Some years later, when I was editing Manzu Islam's novel *Burrow* (2004), a paragraph about the woman, Adela, who agrees to marry the main character to save him from deportation as an illegal immigrant, also brought me up short: 'Her passion in life was betrayal: she wanted to betray her family, her class, her race, her nation and her history. The more she betrayed, the more she felt she had found herself.' Now, I'd met some very voluble Adelas (male and female) at university and was *quite* sure I wasn't like them, but the phrase 'betrayal' was a challenge. As a clergyman's son I'd silently concluded at an early age that I was an atheist; I've always been drawn to support whichever overseas team England was playing – unless it was, during the Apartheid period, the South Africans.

My stance is well known and berated by my nearest and dearest – and responded to publically in an ironic, jokey way – but the truth is that I still have powerful and wholly unintellectual feelings that prevent me from taking pleasure in national triumphs. And yet (*and yet*) I know myself to be deeply English.

Until the age of thirty I'd never been further than camping holidays with my young family in France. At the age of thirty, in 1976, I stepped on a plane that took me to Trinidad and later to Guyana for several months. This was six years after I began research towards a PhD thesis at the University of Leeds concerned with the presence of Indians in the Caribbean, both as writers and as the subject of writing by others. It was nine years before I started Peepal Tree Press in 1985. The months spent researching in Trinidad and Guyana (places I have returned to with increasing frequency in recent years) had two overt purposes: library research for books and documents not available in the UK, and interviews to conduct. But this journey was also to give geographical and human reality to the vast amount of reading I had done. What, of course, the visit also involved was discovering more about myself.

Like most people brought up in a tolerant, socially liberal family from the ethnic majority, I'd never really thought that being white was an integral part of my identity, never, in fact, really thought of myself as being white. In Trinidad that was an impossible evasion. There, whiteness marked me as part of a small, wealthy elite, as I discovered on a later visit when I travelled up to the cocoa country of the hills of North Trinidad with an Indian friend, watching a rumbustious village cricket match. There I was sought out to be thanked for

donating the ground to the village team. This was amusing but in a way more uncomfortable than being abused for my whiteness by an old black man as I walked around the Savannah in Port of Spain.

In Guyana, in 1976, my whiteness marked me out as a kind of ghost, since white Guyanese had all but disappeared from Forbes Burnham's Co-operative Socialist republic. This invisibility put me in situations that were at once immensely valuable for my research, and uncomfortable. As a revenant from a vanished group, African and Indian Guyanese were happy to confide to me their unvarnished, negative and highly stereotyped views about each other.

What was more difficult was the respect, a bowing forehead on your arm, expressed by some older Indians who wanted to tell you how much gratitude they felt to the old estate managers – the Mr Mckenzies and the like – who had treated them 'good', and how much they regretted the departure of the British colonial government who had treated them much better than the current government. This was all uncomfortable stuff to hear. Where were the militant anticolonial workers who had brought Cheddi Jagan to power? (They were there, of course, and I recall a stolid and very minor poet who told me how as a PPP activist he'd kept a Thompson sub-machine gun under the floorboards of his village house at the height of the troubles in the early 1960s.)

The other side of this introduction to whiteness came on the plane to Trinidad, when I'd been eavesdropping on a conversation in deep Trinidadian

Jeremy Poynting
'But England... What do you want with England?

"The walls of the apartment had been hollowed out by insects and flying cockroaches. After incessant rain I was, like Mohan Biswas at Arwacas in *A House for Mr Biswas*, confronted by an alarming invasion of flying ants that had to be swept out in a vast pile."

creole, only to discover that these old-talkers were white. None of these discoveries was a surprise, but the experience of confronting such situations in the flesh is always more powerful than anything you read.

But betrayer of England or not, that visit to the Caribbean forty years ago left me with memories that have been extraordinarily persistent. I remember cotching up in a barracks-like short stay apartment in the hills of St Ann's in Trinidad, right next to the psychiatric hospital and listening to the human howls that disturbed the night. In the mornings, I would fill my pockets with cents to pay passage past the sturdy beggars on day release from the hospital who lined the hill. The walls of the apartment had been hollowed out by insects and flying cockroaches. After incessant rain I was, like Mohan Biswas at Arwacas in *A House for Mr Biswas*, confronted by an alarming invasion of flying ants that had to be swept out in a vast pile. I remember Sita, the pretty young Indian girl (surely an exile from a Samuel Selvon novel), on the run from a violent husband, who wanted to come to cook for me (I resisted), and the Portuguese couple, escapees from an A.H. Mendes story, whose violent rows disturbed the peace.

I remember, too, with deep affection converting a letter acquaintance with the late and very much lamented Anson Gonzalez into a friendship that lasted nearly 40 years until his death. I can still see the duplicating machine in his front room on which he produced *The New Voices*; the country rumshop where he tricked me into drinking a shot of puncheon rum in one gulp; the companionable visit to a calypso tent where I discovered both what impromptu picong was all about and Anson's old reputation as a Don Juan, as confessed in his collection of poems *The Lovesong of Boysie B.*

When I moved on to Guyana, I remember standing with Rooplall Monar in the ruins of the old Lusignan estate, where he had grown up in a mud-floor logie, as he acted out a story about a badbye (bad boy) called Shit-a-lap, one of the characters in the set of stories that became *Backdam People*, the very first book Peepal Tree published. I stayed with Monar in his house in Annandale and whilst I squeamishly resisted the idea of becoming a literal blood brother, we too became close. My only problem with Monar's place was the dread of being taken short and needing the lavatory at night. The fact that it was an outside privy was no problem; it was just that in the pitch blackness you had to cross a deep little trench – almost a canal – by a single narrow and wobbly plank to get there. But sitting gaffing on Monar's verandah with men from the sugar estate (drinking too much rum) and listening to the earthy, heterogeneous and speculative imaginations of these men, I knew how insultingly and snobbishly wrong John Hearne had been when he criticised Wilson Harris's *The Far Journey of Oudin* (1961) for robing his 'innocent and uncaring people in philosophical vestments which they wear about as comfortably as would a navvy dressed in a duke's full coronation regalia.'[1]

For me, as an atheist rationalist, there were the powerful experiences of being present at Kali Mai pujas[2] and at a Cumfa night[3] and witnessing the reality of possession, and how, feeling the possibility of being swept away, I had kept my feet firmly *off* the ground lest the vibrations of the drumming travelled up my body to my brain. I remember a man who previously had been rolling on the ground, barking like a dog, who then addressed me in the most Oxfordian of accents, gently commenting on my caution.

Guyana in 1976 was already seven years into the long twenty-five years of rigged elections and the beginnings of authoritarian party paramountcy and the cult of Comrade Burnham[4], but in 1976 there was still something of a buzz around the idea of decolonisation. The economy had not wholly collapsed, though the signs were there. Returning to Guyana a couple of times in the 1980s I saw the place at its lowest ebb. I remember being asked by a young woman if I would help her carry her too-heavy bag from the plane. Alarm bells went off, but what the bag contained was a massive lump of cheese. When I was first in Annandale, there were only a couple of fishing boats down by the shore; when I returned in the 80s there was a fleet of twenty boats, no signs of fish, and big, well-fed prosperous men walking about the village with the unmistakeable air of self-satisfaction and gentle menace. But there was also the old man who wept on my shoulder because his family had left for North America and he was too old and unskilled to go. As a Marxist socialist, witnessing the collapse of a mimic East European type command economy, this was a valuable lesson. I remain a radical socialist but since then of an increasingly libertarian kind.

Jeremy Poynting

'But England... What do you want with England?

"There's a special smell that hits you as you drive up the East Coast Demerara road: it's a scent with a top-note of a salty, shrimpy, sea-weed and a bottom note of the sweet heavy fumes of molasses from the Lusignan sugar factory. It always makes the hair on the back of my neck stand up."

I have spent time in Jamaica, Barbados, St Lucia, Trinidad, Montserrat, but Guyana still has my heart. There's a special smell that hits you as you drive up the East Coast Demerara road: it's a scent with a top-note of a salty, shrimpy, sea-weed and a bottom note of the sweet heavy fumes of molasses from the Lusignan sugar factory. It always makes the hair on the back of my neck stand up.

I have no illusions about the Caribbean. Along with its stunning and sustained creativity in a variety of art forms, I have seen the dereliction, the raw social and racial divisions and know of the ubiquity of nihilistic violence, which of course goes back to our violence in slavery and colonial days. (I have just recently finished writing an introduction to V.S. Reid's pioneering novel, *New Day* (1949), with its reflections on the colonial state pogrom which slaughtered over five hundred black people after the Morant Bay rebellion of 1865.) But I'm always eager to return, and England always feels especially grey and drab when you come back to it after a Caribbean sojourn – that is until the next weekend when my wife and I put on our hiking boots and head for the Yorkshire Dales.

I've written about my voyage out, but the pleasures of internal exile from narrow Englishness were gained as much from relationships with Caribbean people in the UK, from the young pre-nurses at the FE college in Leeds with whom, almost fifty years ago, I traded sessions on Caribbean history for their superior knowledge of reggae and infectious delight in such slack songs as Max Romeo's 'Wet Dream', to the writers we publish and the people with whom I now work at Peepal Tree.

There isn't space here to analyse the meaning of these fragments of memory in the construction of who I now think I am. The Caribbean has been only one of the journeys. The other began a few years ago when I picked up my long neglected copy of E.P. Thompson's *The Making of the Working Class* and began to pursue its clues to other reading to make connection with a quite different sort of Englishness – to discover Thomas Spence (1750-1814), Olaudah Equiano (1745-1797) not merely as the literary ex-slave but as the English radical in the London Corresponding Society, and the internationalism of the literary and political radical John Thelwall (1764-1834) – and so much more. There's no space either to say more about this discovery of a quite alternative England to the monarchical heritage version I still loathe with a passion (albeit with a weakness for the gardens of the English minor aristocracy). I've more recently been back to George Lamming's *The Pleasures of Exile* (1960) and the treaty he wants between Prospero and Caliban. I thought about what Lamming's essays had to say to me personally rather than as a text consumed in my PhD research, and it reinforced my sense of evasion about keeping the Caribbean and England in different compartments. Recently, at a Harewood House reception, a stately home near Leeds built by the Lascelles family[5] from the profits of financing the slave trade and sugar estates in the Caribbean, Peepal Tree was there as co-partners in a prize established for Black and Asian British women writers. Paulette Morris, a Leeds-born black woman of many talents, also at Peepal Tree, said something forgiving, questioning and wise. You can't undo history she said, but she did resent the absence of anything on display that

accounted for both why Harewood had been built and why she was in Leeds. Therein lay a serious evasion. Harewood was built in the 1760s but visitors were told how in 1840 new money from a marriage had come into the family enabling £20,000 worth of improvements (around £8m in present money) to be undertaken. The money almost certainly came from the £20,000 the Lascelles were granted in compensation for the slaves they had owned after Emancipation.[6] There is much still to disentangle in England's (Britain's) relationship to the Caribbean.

~

When Hewet answers Rachel's question in *The Voyage Out*, 'But England… What do you want with England', his response, 'My friends chiefly… And all the things one does' makes sense to me, if you add family to friends. But what are all the things one does? As I complete writing this piece, a narrow, xenophobic little Englandism seems to have persuaded the English and Welsh electorate that they would be better off out of Europe, which for many meant wanting migrant workers out of England. Resistance has its satisfactions, but just now it's hard as an English man to savour many of the things one does.

I am sure that whatever vitality England possesses has derived both from looking outwards, even though that outward movement has often been at the cruel expense of those with whom we have made contact, and from the inward immigrant flows that have enriched our culture. I see that as true both as a nation and for myself.

W N Herbert

The Dream of the Airport

The car hire company bestows upon you the great gift
of abandoning you to the airport overnight. Returned
to the eternal striplights of your early travels,
you wrap your head in the checkered pakama, place
the green Ethiopian Airways eyemask on your face,
and insert the orange earplugs which can't quite block
the music of The Continuity out – that shuffling of the less
lucky travellers, banging of trays as their diminished
possessions are scanned, ping and pronouncement
of the missing's names by the same old siren. How many
decades have you been passed through here without
ever leaving home? Try escaping into your recurrent dream:
the one about an airport. Then it's four. Abandon sleep
to walk directly through the dream of the airport:
its labyrinth as one bright uncomplicating hall.
Your Minotaur passes, long horns carved with lists,
memoranda, minutiae of the dates he fears. His horns
score both walls at once, his hooves click and chip
this marble. Here's your chance to miss tomorrow
in its role as The Next Episode, to lose the need
for such times to pass, that dumb urgency. Go out
into the night's cool breezes: be glad the bus
which will return you to your place in the action
has not yet arrived. Look up: there are still no birds,
no stars have been allocated to you. You forget, but
this is the hour at which your father died. The night
is like a charcoal horse pacing in its ash paddock –
it chafes itself away as it walks. Walk back into
the long departure hall and pass among the pissed-off
officials, the ecstatic sleepers. We are already within
Asclepius's temple: look, at the opposite end
she's still asleep, the woman you must travel with.
The furniture of your luggage surrounds her like a room
with no walls. She is sleeping in public: we are all
sleeping in public, together, sleeping in public together
forever. Go to her and rewind yourself in the shawl
and pray, your head to her head. The lights keep burning.
Go to her and dream about the airport in the night.

W N Herbert

26th Dolrum

When the ghaists o thi dinged doon
   ur mair real nor thi new-biggit;
when they're nearly mair there as ghaists
   than as yir memory o thum;
when yir dwaums o thi ghaists ur mair real
   nor thi air cut thru the lost stane o thum:
    thi space
          whaur thi sel maun levitate,
whaur thi legs of memory can hae a hing
   and footer fur a footin
             and find nane;
whaur thi fisses o thi deid hae seepit back
   intae pub wallpaper, ilka skin cell
haundit tae a blackdeathwaatch beetle, ivry pore o yir ill-
mindit anes
       donatit til
   a monamaggot i thi hert's sunkenmoncken aumry –

listen tae thi ghaisties o Dundee
i thi doldrums of eftir-yir-aforelife, street-
singin i thi backies wi nae fronts
crehin tae thi windies wi nae gless, nae fremms,

                                  nae waas, nae sterrs

      Eh focht in twa wurld wars
      & Eh'm hung-ry...

Doon comes the manna fae nae man:
twa jeely pieces wrappit in a page fae thi Tully,

                              Extra Ower Late Extra;

   a thruppenny bit fae nae wifie neither:

      Here ye go –
      awa an dinnae sing ony mair.

W N Herbert

27th Dolrum

Fellini fiss oan thi Nummer 73
mune-broch o dyed black herr aroond
yir perfickly medd-upness, fictive Signora o
    thi late fifties tae early seeventies,
bus-pass tae thi Ferry that beh
thi Liz Taylored arc o yir broo
                    shid shairly tak ye tae thi Grand Canal
   or at least thi Dorsoduro, curvin lyk yir spine,
thi bus a vaporetto noo, sliderin
     thru thi decades past
  thi Eastern Necropolis, Diaghilev and Ezra therein,
mascara *maschera* fur thi wintry
festa della nonna in Piazza Santa Margherita,
  an Aperol or an Irn Bru afore ye,
fluttirbeh shades i thi thinnin sun,
                 Peggy Glugginhame

  doon thi Strips o Craigie and up
     past thi *palazzos di iuta*, mooth
a Montalcino o lippie, a Loren-lie calligraphy
   o thi unsaid, thi lang untelt,
      thi niver-comin hame...

W N Herbert

Akládia

Beside the table laden with honey, a little orrery
of off-white, flat-poled cheeses – Anthotiri,
Kefalotiri, Graviera: names as sure as planets' –

at the foot of the steep path from Argyroupoli, or,
toponyms being less secure, the acropolis
of ancient Lappa, or from Ottoman Gaidouropoli,
or Donkey City, on a descendant of which
my daughter once descended, she
white-knuckled on the reins, it
white-hooved on the marble like a cobble chute –

near the necropolis where five virgins, *pente parthénes*,
hid in the rock-hollowed tombs from
our many named and nameless uncertainties
till, by dying, they gave birth to the *pigés* – springs –

across from where she dismounted, from the threshold
of the estiatorio *Ágia Dínami* or Divine Force, selling
LIVE TROUTS, heads slithering in black-green pools,
and the spatchcocked lamb of *Arní Antikristo*,
beneath the first arches of the aqueduct
that would have harvester spider-legged the valley,
smoke doubling the foliage of huge, sun-pierced sycamores:

a box, filled with pears, *akládia*,
green as surprise, stalks upright, like
a herd of breasts, gathered and stockaded.

Beth McDonough

Understanding this poem's watered fabric

She [...] land-patterns palms
to anchor his sea.

Good people sometimes bring our writing
into places we hadn't contemplated, offering a
responsibility, a burden or an opportunity, or
likely a tight twist of all three. In this case, I was
asked to produce a poem about the sea for *Not a
Drop* (Beautiful Dragons). Indeed, oceans pulse
through much of my work, so my poet-friend's
suggestion was hardly strange, just characteristically
kind and impetuous.

If the sea was never a problem, this was not to be
any sea – I had a choice of five remaining bodies
of water, as yet unclaimed by invited writers. No
oceans I'd be swimming in, nor even sailed or
flown across.

Once accepted, even unasked, a commitment is a
commitment.

I decided on the Gulf of Bali, certain I would be
able to spool something from waters round the
islands which gave the world *batik*. Had I not run
plenty of molten wax on papers, on cottons, on
silks? In my mind, I let loose those beautiful
technical words, in themselves already half a
poem – this was a poem I *could* write. I sensed the
crackle of that final dip, enjoyed blue dyes like tides
running deep into cloth. This was a poem I knew I
could write. I understand seas from my long swims,
know their surface tensions, their changes, their
sudden depths. Of *course* I could weave compar-
isons, unravel metaphors. This was a poem I *can*
write. I began...

The closest I have been to Bali is Sri Lanka, where
I have watched women pucker together to deft
extraordinary patterns on unstretched cotton
clenched in their bare hands. By an oil drum of
water over a wood fire, they chatted, fashioned
quick-bordered shapes and patterns, rolled that
last needful wax coat to splinter under the arches
of their unshod feet. Women, very comfortable,
together in their work. Yet this is really nothing
of the poem I *will* write. I started again...

Not so far away, on canvas-sailed boats, their
fisher menfolk pulled out from shore, wrapped in
batik sarongs. Such a fast-drying garment, cool,
yet sun protective, flexible, easily tucked up –
perfect for work on the Indian Ocean. A cloth,
lively and bright with designs of lobsters, prawns,
fish and crabs. Surely Balinese fishermen must
wear something similar? I went to some research
materials and yes, my reading suggests they do. I
wonder: Has this anything to do with my poem?

His is all fish-writhe, curly crustaceans [...], *tjanting*
lines eeled from the shared pot. She sends him
on crackle through waves – all her resist
in the very last skim of that wax.

Those real, handed-down patterns in the cloth are
potent traditional symbols women craft into fabric
to keep their men safe. I understand that part, just
there. That happens much closer to home. But *that*
isn't the poem I'm writing. After all, I know from my
time in Kintyre, and from my own family's Buchan
fabrics and histories, how fisher families have always
feared their keeper sea – kept their own supersti-
tions, made their own shapes and motifs. All this
distracts from the poem I am writing. *Or does it?*

All salt-stiffen from four nights offshore, she
unwraps him [...]
Somewhere this simmer dim she
unsweats him [...]

What is this poem – the one I believe I'm meant
to know?

His is part-Nordic in crosses, in peeries, in noughts.
[...] lines hooked to her belt, through pale nights;
never quite dares to cast off.

Are the Shetland fisher wife and her Balinese sister
doing something so very different as they send their
men out, fit for their oceans on which they depend
and yet fear? Or do they let themselves be bound
in the kit of the practical garments they make,
patterned fast in meaningful designs that have
weathered for centuries? Don't both sets of supersti-
tions twine and wrap around them to the last?

She checks the neck ribs'
close hold, lest he bloat up [...]

These lines are not biddable. These lines want
to loop countries, swim past continents, weave
through languages and memories. These are not
words I intended to write, to fulfil what I thought
or planned, what I filed or knew. These aren't the
lines that knit my up certainties. This is the poem
I don't know. The poem I have yet to find out.

She rubs away gone nights
eases those tucked-in pasts.

I have been neither to Bali nor to Shetland, and
I am unable to write the poem I truly meant to
write.

Yet what is here?

Essay

Amit Chaudhuri

Fredric Jameson's Strange Journey

"It can be an oddly satisfying experience to observe an exponent of 'theory' succumbing suddenly to the precedence of creative activity, either by engaging in it themselves or by paying homage to it."

It can be an oddly satisfying experience to observe an exponent of 'theory' succumbing suddenly to the precedence of creative activity, either by engaging in it themselves or by paying homage to it. The satisfaction involves not so much a sense of *schadenfreude* as some longing we continue to harbour for 'culture', as well as its paradoxical conflation with human nature. Could it be that these theorists are possessed periodically by the same paradoxical longing?

An early instance documenting this particular satisfaction occurs in the young Friedrich Nietzsche, when the world of German romanticism that still holds him in its spell is already waning. But the young man, in *The Birth of Tragedy*, is exercised by another period of transition – in Greek antiquity – when he believes the imaginative passions of Aeschylus and Sophocles gave way to the scepticism and careful rationality of Socrates. And yet, Nietzsche wrote, even Socrates, not long before his death, had to capitulate and surrender to a realm of experience – the arts – he had previously shut out:

> As he explains to his friends in prison, often one and the same dream apparition came to him, always with the words, 'Socrates, practise music!'... Finally in prison he came to understand how, in order to relieve his conscience completely, to practise that music which he had considered insignificant...

> ... That statement of Socrates's dream vision is the single indication of his thinking about something perhaps beyond the borders of his logical nature. So he had to ask himself: Have

I always labelled unintelligible things I could not understand? Perhaps there is a kingdom of wisdom which is forbidden to the logician?[1]

More recently, Ranajit Guha, whose writings once transformed postcolonial historiography, intrigued and scandalised admirers by publishing a book, *History at the Limit of World-History*, in which he, in effect, asked fellow-historians to look beyond the discipline of history, with its 'statist' intentions, toward literature and its enshrining of 'wonder'.[2] It's tempting to see this as another 'late' Socratic moment, for Guha was eighty two years old when this book appeared. 'Late style', for Edward Said[3], brought to the work of some artists an enriching intransigence and contrariness; but lateness, in theorists, occasionally manifests itself as a form of self-questioning, an ambivalence about the materialism that shaped their critiques. 'I present these observations in the form of an autocritique,' (*HLW* 74) says Guha disarmingly.

For him, the continuing problem with history is the way it privileges elevated 'statist' preoccupations (for this, says Guha, Hegel is culpable) over the everyday – whose significance was pointed out by Heidegger. It's the everyday, and a sense of wonder in relation to it, that Guha draws attention to in his short book. From 'fact', the currency of the historian, he turns to the Heideggerian coinage 'facticity', where the thing in question possesses not just empirical veracity but an ' "innerworldly"... being in the world' (*HLW* 79).

Guha offers to the reader not Heidegger as an exemplary proponent of wonder, but the poet, 'Rabindranath Tagore, the greatest South Asian writer of our age'. In particular, Guha draws our attention to an essay, 'Historicality in Literature' ('*Sahitye Aitihasikata*') that's actually a transcript of remarks contained in a letter written by Tagore to the younger poet and critic Buddhadeva Bose two weeks before his death. Attacked for decades from several sides by modernists like Bose, by Marxist critics for not being enough of a modern, or for not grappling with politics head on, Tagore chose to come clean, and to say outright that, for him, poetry had primacy over history: 'I have heard it said again and again that we are guided altogether by history, and I have energetically nodded, so to say, in my mind whenever I heard it. I have settled this debate in my own head where I am nothing but a poet' (Guha's translation; *HLW* 96).

Tagore enumerated three epiphanies he had as a boy in Calcutta that marked him out, in his own eyes, for the vocation of poetry. The first was noticing light fall in the morning on 'the trembling coconut fronds in the courtyard' as 'the dewdrops burst into glitter'; the second involved seeing 'a dark cumulus suspended high above the third storey of our house'; the third, witnessing a 'cow licking the back of a foal with the affection reserved usually for her own calf' (*HLW* 77). 'I have it in my mind to say, "Off with your history!"'[4] wrote Tagore to Bose, as he posited these three images of the everyday against it. Guha invokes Tagore's refutation of one kind of materialism (history) on behalf of another (the commonplace) to question the limits of his own lifelong investment in theory.

Amit Chaudhuri

Fredric Jameson's Strange Journey

"In this, he is not unlike Said and Derrida and a whole host of other mostly very well known critics and philosophers who began as critics of canonical authors and never really relinquished that role. 'Creative' writers who practise serious criticism have, for long, provoked an old romantic suspicion in post-Enlightenment cultures."

The 'late' moments, described by the writers and philosophers Jacques Derrida and Edward Said, occurred not necessarily as a change of heart towards the literary, but as doubts expressed over their work's legacy: Derrida's dismay over 'deconstructivism', with its vulgarised scepticism, in sections of academia; Said's disillusionment with the professionalised postcolonial industry. Neither had to turn publicly towards the literary or the 'high' arts because both – like many of the theorists from the sixties onwards engaged in dismantling these entities – had already had a lifelong and profound engagement with the arts. Derrida had identified something called 'Western metaphysics' as the enemy, and Said had named Western imperialism as his. The imaginative practices that were enmeshed in these now dubious parameters had to be casualties, notwithstanding the fact that the discredited institution of literature continued to nourish both Said and Derrida.

Although critical theory and post-modernity announced not only the death of the author but the passing of what Fredric Jameson, in *The Modernist Papers*,[5] refers to as 'affect' (roughly the equivalent of aesthetic emotion, or what Guha, borrowing from Sanskrit poetics, calls *rasa*), it would appear that rumours of the death may have been exaggerated. For Jameson, this is clear from the dates of the essays in *The Modernist Papers*, and the preoccupations of his other work; the study of literature has been formative and inescapable. In this, he is not unlike Said and Derrida and a whole host of other mostly very well known critics and philosophers who began as critics of canonical authors and never really relinquished that role. 'Creative' writers who practise serious criticism have, for long, provoked an old romantic suspicion in post-Enlightenment cultures. Yet, for about four decades, we've been living in an age not of literature but of theory, and the question must be, if not reversed, at least parodied.

The question concerns not so much whether theorists have led a double life, as some poets famously have (as bankers, insurance brokers, professors), but why the doubleness in whose form literature has been available to them – as repressive political construct and an area of disruptive play – hasn't been sufficiently addressed. It's not just that literature hasn't gone away; literature has also to be engaged with and understood through this quality of doubleness that it probably always possessed.

Jameson's eloquent (and often shrewd) work on postmodernism has been informed by at least two locations, if we can call epochs and phases in intellectual history locations, and by, as I've suggested, a not wholly acknowledged doubleness. Born spiritually into modernism, Jameson found himself, in the early eighties, in a foreign country – post-modernity – from which there was evidently no return. Marxism provided him with a language ('late capitalism') with which to understand, historically, the features of this baffling new country's culture ('postmodernism').[6]

Jameson, besides possessing a remarkable sense both of distance and of the momentous, also cultivated a crucial intellectual acceptance of the fact of literary and intellectual exile. He first encountered this country not as a horizon, a map, or a nation with boundaries, but as a simultaneously shrunken and expansive version of geographies he'd known before, describing it in *Postmodernism* as 'a total space, a complete world, a kind of miniature city' (*P* 40) which happened to be the 'inner space' of the Bonaventure Hotel in Los Angeles. Like most émigrés, Jameson experienced his new country of domicile in terms of its physical continuum (space) and what defines space – movement, and habitation (architecture) – while also realising with a shock, as émigrés do, that space here behaved differently from space in the old country:

> I am more at a loss when it comes to conveying the thing itself, the experience of space you undergo when you step off such allegorical devices [elevators and escalators] into the lobby or atrium, with its great central column, surrounded by a miniature lake, the whole positioned between the four symmetrical residential towers with their elevators... I am tempted to say that such space makes it impossible for us to use the language of volume or volumes any longer, since these last are impossible to seize. (*P* 42-3)

Jameson is well aware, of course, that, in the old country from which he's an exile, there's a continuity between space, architecture, habitation, literature (his primary subject of study) and representation; for instance, Heidegger, in his essay on Hölderlin, writes of the metaphors used in relation to poetic language being a habitation, a way of housing 'being'. Yet, in the new country, Jameson knows those continuities don't hold: not only are buildings and spaces *not* a metaphor for literary language here, in the country called 'post-modernity' it's

Amit Chaudhuri

Fredric Jameson's Strange Journey

"If one were to pursue this analogy between the certainties of the familiar on the one hand, and the perils of travel and complex forms of domicile on the other, one would have to admit that, if post-modernity is or was a country, it was a unique one, demanding a special, even unprecedented, allegiance, in that it did not allow for the experiences of exile or nostalgia."

impossible to posit a difference between space as metaphor and space as reality: 'such space makes it impossible for us to use the language of volume or volumes any longer...' (*P* 42-3)

If one were to pursue this analogy between the certainties of the familiar on the one hand, and the perils of travel and complex forms of domicile on the other, one would have to admit that, if post-modernity is or was a country, it was a unique one, demanding a special, even unprecedented, allegiance, in that it did not allow for the experiences of exile or nostalgia. Modernity, of course, was defined by exile and so, probably, was every age before it. But what exactly – besides dinosaurs and the Neolithic man – occurred 'before' modernity? As Jameson points out in *A Singular Modernity*[7] (and this idea itself is not a new one), 'modernity', as a concept and a specific threat, appeared at the beginning of time to the Greeks, who complained bitterly about it. The Hindus, too, were unequivocal about it, and called it *kaliyuga*, or the Dark Age – the epoch in which the sundering of man, governance, and politics on the one hand, and God on the other is absolute and complete.

At a second glance, though, we notice that this hoary but influential bit of periodisation (*kaliyuga*), although seemingly referring to the future, the imminent, or to an age that's only *just* arrived, is actually already always present. *Kaliyuga* begins at the beginning of recorded time and is history itself; there is no record from any previous, more pristine and ethical age. This pretty much indicates that human beings all over have suffered, for millennia, from what Harold Bloom termed 'belatedness'[8]:

a sense of being born at the wrong place at the wrong time, of having missed out on one's truly appointed epoch by decades or even centuries.

If post-modernity is a country, then, it's a country, at least from the eighties onward, populated and shaped entirely by exiles, in that none of the chief theorists or promulgators of what Jameson calls 'full post-modernity' was actually born into it. The exiles made it a point to outlaw any nostalgia for 'home' under the new regime. Nostalgia didn't just become an offence; the ban on it became an astute and new philosophical strategy.

In 'Against Belatedness' in the *London Review of Books* in 1983, Richard Rorty confessed with apparent relief: 'It is to the credit of such post-Heideggerian philosophers as Derrida and Foucault that they avoid this insistence on the belatedness of the modern age.'9 Of course, the modernists, too, like the post-modernists, had acknowledged the impossibility and the misguided nature of the desire to return to the past albeit, unlike the post-modernists, they saw the past as a source of value. But the modernists also realised that a total disavowal of the cultural hoard, of tradition, was equally impossible, and so decided to approach it, tragically, through the luminous fragment – what Jameson describes in *The Modernist Papers* as an aesthetic of 'failure': that is, a preference for partial over total knowledge; a rejection of mastery; an embrace of the transient over the permanent, of the decaying over the finished. For the theorists of post-modernity, however, this aesthetic of failure became morally untenable because of modernism's links to elitism and fascism.

To continually affirm, then, the present in complex, multiple ways, to claim to feel at home in this new condition of domicile in an interconnected world, became one of the principal means of critiquing the transgressions of history. Post-modernity is an unprecedented state (and I'm consciously punning on that word); it was defined entirely by exiles but it has no place for the exile's experience of unease, no recourse for memorialising the past and the journey made from it, and few valid avenues through which to explore past attachments (for example, for the avant garde, prose style, poetry, lyricism or montage).

Does this mean that the theorist in post-modernity never feels any affinity with, or yearning for, the old country, modernity, or any alienation from where they find themselves at present? That this isn't true is suggested by the fact that every other post-modernist must have once been, on the evidence of their deep but ambivalent enthusiasms – phenomenology, literature – a passionate modernist. In Jameson's case, it's his compelling style that reminds us of the exiled modernist pulsating within the domiciled post-modern; and style, as Jameson points out, is supposed to be dead in post-modernity.

The insistence that exile, alienation, and belatedness are dated, then, seems not so much a post-modern pretence or stance, but a complicated, even moving, form of irony, an affecting strategy for moral and intellectual survival in the new climate. It's this irony and instinct for survival, and not just a recognition of the new, that permeates, for instance, Jameson's apotheosis of the Bonaventure Hotel, and makes it shine even today. Jameson sees that it's

Amit Chaudhuri

Fredric Jameson's Strange Journey

"There's an air of fictionality
and absoluteness too – the
emigrant who's gone native
will always partly invent the
new home country, and regard
it as a final abode.

It must be that trajectory of
exile that moves us, then, when
we witness the likes of Derrida,
Said, Guha, or Jameson confront – each in their own way
– that special language called
'literary language'."

better to plunge into the new country rather than
live emotionally in the old one; his description of
the hotel performs this decision beautifully.
As we follow Jameson, in *The Modernist Papers*,
studying the canonical writers of modernism –
Joyce, Proust, Williams, Baudelaire, Rimbaud,
Mallarmé – struggling, over the years, to define
what distinguishes modernism from postmodernism, we see that there's a curious heroism to
the theorists of post-modernism: to their embrace
of the present, their critique of the past, their
reconciliation to the finality of post-modernity, and
to the fact that there's no going back.

Jameson's book has no single thread or argument;
what unifies the 'papers' or essays within it is this
heroic struggle, which gives the writing a distinctive
complexity and resistance – the obsessive urge to
return to these writers, coupled with an equally
obsessive desire to avoid a tone of 'belatedness'.
This is not a tragic heroism, because tragedy isn't a
mode available to, or permissible within, post-
modernity. But there's an illuminating irony –
indeed, a silence – here, which makes strangely
resonant the disavowals of the last forty years.
There's an air of fictionality and absoluteness
too – the emigrant who's gone native will always
partly invent the new home country, and regard
it as a final abode.

It must be that trajectory of exile that moves
us, then, when we witness the likes of Derrida,
Said, Guha, or Jameson confront – each in their
own way – that special language called 'literary
language'. For to live in 'full post-modernity' was
to be conscious, in a more pointed way than ever

before, of the limits of what it's possible to think or say. In his preface to *A Singular Modernity*, Jameson had magisterially observed that it would be dangerous to return, or 'regress', to 'the sentimental idealism of the various ideologies of aesthetic justification'.

Nevertheless, Pierre Macherey, in more than one sense a contemporary of Jameson's, published a paper in 2007 in *Diacritics*, reflecting on the persistent power of literature, which he chose to term, eponymously, 'the literary thing'.[10] The paper, he clarified, 'does not pretend to have the final word on the thing but at the very most to stammer out some initial words' ('TLT' 29). Pierre Bourdieu, Macherey says, has given us something very valuable – an acute idea of the indisputable materiality of literature: that is, literature as 'literary production' and a 'field'. But there was also, Macherey reminds us, the relatively obscure but transgressive Maurice Blanchot, who had argued for literature as a 'space', and for 'the primordial value of the work' ('TLT' 25, 28) coming alive in the reader. Blanchot prompts Macherey to reflect that 'The Literary Thing' is not only a production, but that it 'itself produces' ('TLT' 29), generating further expression from expression. This – as an argument for literature – is an extraordinary thing for a Marxist-formalist-structuralist to say, even stammer.

By some coincidence, a few months before Macherey's article appeared, the Oxford academic Peter D McDonald published 'Ideas of the Book and Histories of Literature: After Theory' in the *PMLA Journal*,[11] where he too set up a contrast between Bourdieu's materialist legacy and the alternative offered by Blanchot. McDonald called the position that Bourdieu and other materialists espoused 'sceptical antiessentialism' ('TLT' 218); while Blanchot was described not as a naive realist or a romantic, but chief amongst the 'enchanted antiessentialists' ('TLT' 219) – someone, in other words, who was disabused of the notion of literature as a universally valid entity, while still accepting that its creative possibilities were transformative. For McDonald, part of the problem with the sceptics was their misreading of Derrida's injunction in his *Grammatalogie*, *'Il n'y a pas de hors-texte.'* The misreading begins, says McDonald, with Gayatri Spivak's famously unambiguous translation: *'There is nothing outside of the text'.* ('TLT' 222)

What Macherey and McDonald seem to suggest is that there's a way of addressing literature as a vital category that exceeds its material formation, without being accused of old-fashioned naivety – even stupidity. Jameson, defining postmodernism, had decided this was no longer possible. Exhibiting the closest he's come to tragic resignation, he'd called pastiche the characteristic literary mode of post-modernity. Pastiche is 'speech in a dead language', it is parody without the subversive humour, 'blank parody, a statue with blind eyeballs' – everything, in its domain, becomes a quotation. Jameson, echoing Paul de Man in *A Singular Modernity* suggests that any 'naive and representational immediacy ("the poem is about nature")' in literature is a myth (*SM, 107*). So we're on familiar post-modern terrain, where to long for affect in literary lan-

Amit Chaudhuri

Fredric Jameson's Strange Journey

guage – a sense of fullness and 'immediacy' - in the arts is to give in to nostalgia. We're left, then, with pastiche.

Yet do pastiche and affect have to be incompatible with each other, as the exiles from modernity claimed so strenuously? Maybe not. And perhaps this is what Jameson is really arguing for in *The Modernist Papers*. Certainly, in other cultures and ages, the self-reflexivity of pastiche and the fullness of affect have happily cohabited in one space. The late AK Ramanujan, the Indian poet, translator, and scholar of Indian antiquity, points out, for instance, that 'all later *Ramayanas*' – the Hindu epic, available in many versions – 'play on the knowledge of previous tellings'. His 'favourite' example of this kind of 'play' is from the 16th-century *Adhyatma Ramayana*, in which the god Rama, upon facing banishment, tells his wife Sita that he doesn't want her to accompany him to the forest. At first, says Ramanujan, Sita counters this with 'the usual arguments: she is his wife, she should share his sufferings, exile herself in his exile and so on.' When none of this works, she is 'furious... and bursts out, "Countless *Ramayanas* have been composed before this. Do you know of one where Sita doesn't go with Rama to the forest?" That clinches the argument...' [12] Self-reflexivity, one presumes, didn't preclude the 16th-century audience from partaking of affect, aesthetic pleasure, or even devotion. Besides, Ramanujan's example isn't really an instance of parody but of a humane joy that embraces self-reflexivity as one of the many circumstances of divinity.

There are examples closer to our time from Western modernity. The Portuguese poet Fernando Pessoa became famous posthumously for the 'heteronyms' – multiple poetic personalities, each with a small oeuvre to his name – he'd invented in secret. Jameson, in passing, places Pessoa, in *The Modernist Papers,* within the 'unfurling of a wave of modern irony over late nineteenth-century European culture' and its aftermath, in which lies 'the relativism of newer playwrights like Pirandello or the point-of-view poets like Fernando Pessoa, with their multitudinous personae' (*MP*, 307). The best known of these personae are Ricardo Reis (celebrated in a Jose Saramago novel), a minor poet of some formal accomplishment; a Whitman-esque urban poet, Álvaro de Campos; and the nature poet and mystic, Alberto Caeiro. Of these, the invention of Caeiro, the first of the heteronyms, was particularly momentous to Pessoa. What began as an intended joke – 'to invent,' as Pessoa wrote in his notebook, 'a bucolic poet... and present him... as if he were a real entity' – became, when Caeiro finally surfaced in his consciousness, something else: 'It was the triumphal day of my life and I will never have anything like it... Excuse me for the absurdity of the expression: my master appeared in me.' [13] The force of this recounted occasion is comparable, then, to the one that Guha cites – the transforming instants in Tagore's life in the Calcutta of his boyhood that set him apart for poetry. The difference is that Caeiro is a fiction, Tagore isn't.

Yet when we look again at the eighty-year-old Tagore's phrasing as he describes the occasion, we find it curious. More than once, Tagore slips from first to third person, and back to the first: for instance, 'But in the history of that day there was no one other than myself who saw those clouds in the quite the same way as I did ... Rabindranath happened to be all by himself in that instance'; and 'In the entire history of that day it was Rabindranath alone who witnessed the scene with enchanted eyes. This I know for certain.' (*HLW*, 88). This is at once grandiose and touching; but it also gives to 'Rabindranath' the aura of a fiction, of a persona coming into being at the moment of confession and self-awareness. Can the dramatic monologue, pastiche, and religiosity then weave into each other? Can one, in the domain of the poetic, be spontaneous and knowing, innocent and performative, at once? Caeiro's 'The Keeper of Sheep'[14] is a simple and luminous sequence about living austerely in the beauties of the physical world: it is the work of a naive poet who precedes history. On the other hand, however, it is full of history and argument, an intellection of a specifically dissenting, romantic, anti-intellectual kind: 'There is enough metaphysics in the world in not thinking about the anything' (*KS*, 115); '"Inner constitution of things".../ "inner sense of the Universe".../ That is all wrong, that is meaningless.' What's sacred is the reality that's most immediate to the senses: 'I don't believe in God because I have never seen him.' (*KS*, 17) 'What matters is knowing how to see,' declares Caeiro. In spite of this, the sequence has few particulars, and deals intriguingly, and radically, in categories and generalities:

I saw that there is no Nature,
That Nature does not exist,

That there are hills, valleys, plains,
That there are trees, flowers, grasses,
That there are rivers and stones... (*KS*, 115)

This conviction – about nature not existing – doesn't prevent Caeiro, at the very end of the sequence, from making a huge, even reckless, assertion: 'Anyway, I was the only Nature poet.' A poetic persona is neither a dramatic voice nor a character in a novel; it has neither a history nor a psychology that we are already privy to, and nor are its views made relative by the presence and views of other characters. We are, in the end, not so much being asked to believe in the plausibility of Caeiro, in the way we are asked to believe in, say, Levin as a character in *Anna Karenina*. We are being asked to believe in the plausibility of his utterances. Most readers would agree that Caeiro has earned his right to say, 'Anyway, I was the only true Nature poet', and would surrender to his prophecy. Yet all readers also know that Caeiro does not exist 'outside of the text'. In so knowing we feel ourselves to be in the 'out there' of reading – that place that is literature itself.

Jane Goldman

Discovery Woolf

"There is a delicious delicacy, a tenuous skepticism to this sense of discovery, which bridges different kinds of finding, observing and knowing, and encompassing both feeling and reason. She writes not simply, 'I had made a discovery', but rather 'I *felt* that I had made a discovery'"

'I felt that I had made a discovery.' Virginia Woolf writes of one of the three 'exceptional moments' or 'moments of being' that she chooses in her carefully drafted late memoir, 'A Sketch of the Past'(1940),[1] to explain 'the strongest pleasure known to her': 'It is the rapture I get when in writing I seem to be discovering what belongs to what; making a scene come right; making a character come together.' (*MB* 80) Writing that very sentence effects a discovery process 'in writing': Woolf discovers her process of discovery 'in writing' it. There is a delicious delicacy, a tenuous skepticism to this sense of discovery, which bridges different kinds of finding, observing and knowing, and encompassing both feeling and reason. She writes not simply, 'I had made a discovery', but rather 'I *felt* that I had made a discovery', a skepticism about the entire relations between subject and object of discovery that brings one to the brink of an *encounter*: an investigative meeting with something already fully present, already shaping and causing feelings of discovery in the apparent discoverer. And it is from such self-conscious reflections that Woolf writes the following passage, often cited as her last attempt at an artistic credo:

> From this I reach what I might call a philosophy; at any rate it is a constant idea of mine; that behind the cotton wool is hidden a pattern; that we—I mean all human beings—are connected with this; that the whole world is a work of art; that we are parts of the work of art. Hamlet or a Beethoven quartet is the truth about this vast mass that we call the world. But there is no Shakespeare, there is no Beethoven; certainly and emphatically there is no God;

we are the words; we are the music; we are the thing itself. And I see this when I have a shock. (*MB* 81)

This atheistic declaration, anticipating later literary critical and theoretical declarations by Roland Barthes and Michel Foucault on the death of the author, is all the more powerful for the context in which she writes it: the very brink of war. (The memoir goes on to record how months later 'The battle is at its crisis; every night the Germans fly over England; it comes closer to this house daily.' *MB* 111) There is much to contemplate here concerning Woolf's understanding of the world as collectively authored text in which we all - 'all human beings' - participate, and not least the implicit feminism at work in undermining the patriarchal authority of God, Shakespeare, and Beethoven as the grounding fathers of that text. But what motivates my own return to this late Woolfian voyage of discovery is the compositional methodology she makes available in her account of that exceptional moment of being:

I was looking at the flower bed by the front door; 'That is the whole,' I said. I was looking at a plant with spread leaves; and it seemed suddenly plain that the flower itself was a part of the earth; that a ring enclosed what was the flower; and that was the real flower; part earth; part flower. It was a thought I put away as being likely to be very useful to me later. (*MB* 80)

'Flower' is intensely repeated here. I marvel at its re-planting in such rhythmic expansion after the initial appearance of 'the flower bed'; how a thought is plucked out of context, yet trails an enclosing 'ring' of context with it. Reflecting on Woolf's insistence that this discovery of the processes of discovery, encapsulated by the childhood unearthing of the flower as 'part earth; part flower', will (and did) in the future become

a revelation of some order; it is a token of some real thing behind appearances; and I make it real by putting it into words. It is only by putting it into words that I make it whole; this wholeness means that it has lost its power to hurt me; it gives me, perhaps because by doing so I take away the pain, a great delight to put the severed parts together. Perhaps this is the strongest pleasure known to me. (*MB* 81)

So in composing the poem, 'Discovery Woolf', I set out on a voyage into Woolf's language to 'make real' her discoveries, to discover how often and in what context she writes the word 'discovery' and its fellow travellers (permutations of 'discoverer' and 'discovery'). In every instance I plucked from her fiction, diaries and her manifestos, I made sure to trail an enclosing ring of language —'part earth; part flower'. The complete poem comprises three voyages. The first, 'Voyage A', journeys through Woolf's ten published novels from *The Voyage Out* (1915) to *Between the Acts* (1941);[2] the second, 'Voyage B', takes its chronological line of discovery of 'discovery' through Woolf's six volumes of posthumously published journals and diaries, spanning the years 1908 to 1941; the third, 'Voyage C', charts a line of discovery through

Jane Goldman

Discovery Woolf

her two major manifestos, *A Room of One's Own*
(1929) and *Three Guineas* (1938). This 'Discovery
Woolf' triptych is of course only a recce, a pilot
mission of sorts. Only 'Voyage A'is reproduced
here.

The ten stanzas of 'Voyage A' chart Woolf's
'discoveries' in each of her ten novels. How
satisfying that Woolf's debut novel, *The Voyage Out*
(1915), whose title may allude to the best-seller,
The Voyage of 'The Discovery' (1905) by the
explorer Robert Falcon Scott (1868-1912) on his
successful Antarctic expedition of 1902-1904, is
studded with the word 'discovery' and its variants.
The ostensible destination of the sea-voyage in
this novel is a fictional British colony on a South
American island. But there is little attempt at
realism here. Woolf, in her diary,[3] understood her
achievement to be 'a harlequinade', an 'assortment
of patches' (*D2* 17), and the reader is indeed
launched onto a turbulent sea of allusions and
citations to numerous canonical literary texts,
many of which point to dark allegories of sexual
violence, rape, imperialism and death.

The deployment of the word 'discovery' and its
variants in Woolf's *The Voyage Out* moves from a
sense of being 'startled by this discovery', through
a series of constructions that point up gender, race,
class and sexual politics at work in the inscription
of subjects and objects to a sense of thwarted
discovery, a harbinger of the cruel death of its
young protagonist: 'dull to die before they have
discovered'. It is only by voyaging further into the
numerous works which *The Voyage Out* cites in its
patchwork of often fugitive literary allusions that

the reader may begin to 'account for the nature of shock administered by Rachel's abrupt and untimely death', as Jim Stewart wisely observes of his own erudite uncovering of 'a pervasive network of references to Greco-Roman literature' in that novel.[4]

How poignant that the word appears only once in her fifth novel, *To the Lighthouse* (1927)[5]: 'only in the moment of discovery'. In this novel, which Woolf understood as a form of elegy, Scott's ill-fated and thwarted Antarctic expedition of 1912 is famously employed as a metaphor for the intellectual failings of the philosopher Mr. Ramsay. For Ramsay, who is deluded by qualities 'that in a desolate expedition across the icy solitudes of the Polar region would have made him the leader, the guide, the counselor' (*TL* 57), seems to be reflecting on Scott's tragic Polar mission as analogy for his own limited reputation, a 'leader of a doomed expedition' of another more abstract kind:

> Who then could blame the leader of that forlorn party which after all has climbed high enough to see the waste of the years and the perishing of stars, if before death stiffens his limbs beyond the power of movement he does a little consciously raise his numbed fingers to his brow, and square his shoulders, so that when the search party comes they will find him dead at his post, the fine figure of a soldier? Mr. Ramsay squared his shoulders and stood very upright by the urn. (*TL* 60)

If Mr. Ramsay's portrait makes the reader worry that 'discovery' is always a boy's game, how

startlingly laid bare are the gender politics of 'discovery' two years later in Woolf's *A Room of One's Own*[6] : 'Columbus discovered America' and 'Newton discovered the laws of gravitation' (*AROO* 85) and 'new facts are bound to be discovered' (*AROO* 91). These are in stark contrast to her observations on and to her audience of young women: 'you have never made a discovery' (*AROO* 112).

How disturbing that the only one of Woolf's novels to be entirely without the word 'discovery' is her posthumously published tenth and final work, *Between the Acts* (1941). Here (in Stanza 10) I have charted instances in that text of words that begin with its first two syllables but turn into other utterances that disappoint the word 'discovery'. These are: 'disconnectedly [...] discordant [...] discourse [...] discord [...] discordantly'. Yet even in the close context of my fragmentary samplings, we may see an optimism in these discordances ('if discordant, producing harmony'). We might take further courage for future voyages into Woolf's writings. On the 15th of January 1941, two months before her suicide, Woolf's diary reflects, as it happens, on news that ' [James] Joyce is dead' (*D5* 352). She rediscovers her thoughts on how she first read *Ulysses*: 'I think with spasms of wonder, of discovery' (*D5* 353). So too, reading Woolf, on 1st June 2016, I think with spasms of wonder, of discovery.

Jane Goldman

Discovery Woolf: Voyage A

1.
startled by this discovery
discovered a card, which he planked down
one might discover a new reptile
about the discoveries in Crete
wasn't it Wilde who discovered the fact
the discovery was very welcome
it was discovered that a long line of ants
enjoy the fruits of the discovery
discovery of a terrible possibility
discovering that they knew some of the same
discovered really beautiful things
did not discover that they possessed names
talk into these quarters she might discover
had discovered that she had taken up
whatever discoveries were made there
was one discovery which could not be
discover what sort of person she was
discovered that one of the grey coils
discovered that six people really wished the same
a moment undiscovered, they were seen
leaning, without fear of discovery
I've discovered the way to get Sancho
she tried to discover why he was uneasy
never been discovered to possess names
dull to die before they have discovered

2.
the first time, or making discoveries
discover his own handwriting suddenly
distressing search a fresh discovery
discovered I was related to the poet
this state of things had been discovered
Celia has discovered that Cyril is married
but life — the process of discovering

not the discovery itself at all
but life — the process of discovering
not the discovery itself at all
the process of discovery was life
her priceless discovery, a young man
discovered that she never made an ugly
bedroom door on a mission of discovery
she felt came only from the discovery
this discovery of hers must show traces
discovery is that he owned a house
discover was the truth of what she herself
consequences of the discovery
speedily found, her discoveries gave her
discover what your feeling is for her
flinched and roused herself, and discovered
as you've all discovered each other's faults
unhappy laughter of monkeys, they discovered
his experiences, his discovery
because his discovery was so important
discover what they had said of him now
probably because she's discovered something
failed to discover the work they were in search of
surface of the sea, which could be discovered
she was astonished at her discovery
yet with strange hope, too, the discovery
discover the two figures in the window.

3.
discovered the lines which he had been seeking
end of dinner, the new discovery
it is surely a great discovery
to swim in finger-bowls was discovered
in mule carts to discover the sources
she had discovered something—something very

Jane Goldman

Discovery Woolf: Voyage A

4.
a marvellous discovery indeed —
music should be visible was a discovery
for no reason that she could discover
great discoveries; how there is no death
5.
even in the moment of discovery

6.
frequent discovery of the skeletons
in the ardour of this discovery
dome which her eyes had first discovered so
discovering that they were of the same sex
only suppose that some new discovery
great discovery of marriage proceeded
step by step, to submit to the new discovery,
discovered at once—to pass its examination
service he may discover for himself

7.
discoverers of an unknown land
bound, surely, to discover my desire
I discover a new vein in myself I
in a bran-pie to discover my self
not Neville, a wonderful discovery
what other discovery will there be?

8.
Flush soon discovered, are strictly divided
your accomplices as I can discover —
you I have discovered and will never lose
delighting in the discoveries she made, so

Flush too was making his discoveries
    in their voyages of discovery —
            soon discovered that he could make them
              discovered a world that she had never

    9.
              The discovery annoyed her. It proved Ellen
    a perpetual discovery, my life. A miracle.

    10.
            disconnectedly, she explained
          if discordant, producing harmony—
had lost the thread of his discourse.
  or do they introduce a discord . . . Ding
    birds syllabling discordantly life, life, life, with
out measure, without stop devouring the tree.

Art

Reinhard Behrens

Expeditions into Naboland

"Fed by my further travels, both real and imagined, Naboland has materialised in drawings, paintings, prints and installations, generating a parallel world to the one observed."

While working for the German Archaeological Institute on the Turkish West coast in 1975 I came across a newspaper article that reported the collision between a Turkish submarine and a cargoship with the name NABOLAND. In the previous year I came upon a little metal toy submarine on the German North Sea coast. This found object and the name 'Naboland' gave me the idea of an imaginative voyage: a little tin traveller venturing into the unknown territory of Naboland. This has remained my artistic occupation ever since that chance encounter forty years ago. Fed by my further travels, both real and imagined, Naboland has materialised in drawings, paintings, prints and installations, generating a parallel world to the one observed.

In 1979 and with the help of a German Academic Exchange Grant, I arrived in Scotland. My fledgling project was given a new boost by what I took to be the whimsical appreciation of the delectably quirky and oblique in British culture that gave my Naboland travels a constant source of replenishment. In my regular outings with the Edinburgh University Mountaineering Club, the landscape and splendour of the Scottish Highlands also provided an on-going source of inspiration, given that my Hamburg childhood was lived in a comparatively flat terrain. Excursions in winter time in Scotland made it easy to pretend to be one of Scott's desperate party searching for the pole.

My work reflects this exposure to the elements in a series of etchings of which *Marooned on the Ice-Floe* is an example. Its central shape is that

"The work thus simulates an
exhibit from a museum of polar
exploration. However, because
of its reduced scale, suggesting
also the child-sized proportions
of its absent and fictitious
explorers, visitors that peer into
this imaginary scientific survival
hut temporarily vacated by
its diminutive inhabitants are
turned into voyeuristic giants."

of a raft – one that I had built with real materials for a previous exhibition. Surrounding the
raft that actually appears stuck in ice are visual
references to the history of arctic exploration
that I came across in antiquarian bookshops, the
latter providing a treasure trove of imagery for
my drawings and etchings ever since. The arctic
appearance of the Scottish mountains in winter
led to my fascination with the Inuit who until
recently managed to live in harmony with their
surroundings without producing any waste on
the edge of terrain barely habitable to humans.

Arctic Hut, created as a centre piece for many of my
exhibitions, contains genuine old elements such as
driftwood, rope, tins, laboratory fittings, photographs and crockery; a real crackling radio hints
at signs of real life, adding to the forlorn atmosphere. The work thus simulates an exhibit from a
museum of polar exploration. However, because
of its reduced scale, suggesting also the child-sized
proportions of its absent and fictitious explorers,
visitors that peer into this imaginary scientific
survival hut temporarily vacated by its diminutive
inhabitants are turned into voyeuristic giants.

Whenever I assemble my *Arctic Hut* as part of a
wider Naboland installation, I always envisage
arctic explorers who having reached a hostile
shore, need to hastily build a shelter for the night
before the weather closes in, or before the polar
bears return. My cardboard boxes and the various
objects in my constructions very much resemble
those wooden boxes hoisted onto the ice that
can be seen in so many photographs of the early
arctic explorers.

Reinhard Behrens

Expedition into Naboland

Whilst I have a now familiar set of wooden beams and planks, tarpaulin and rope, all weathered on the sea shore of the Firth of Forth, I never follow a fixed plan but enjoy the thrill of improvising my structures with the given elements as a creative process. In this selfish pursuit, there is always the precious moment when all carefully placed objects, dated articles of scientific research, maps, cutlery, darned socks, jubilee mugs, diaries, glass jars and tools build a momentum of their own, generating a spark of life and purposefulness that brings magic back again. Having restored the soul of the hut once again I quickly withdraw from my work, not to startle the returning diminutive explorers who might have spent their day measuring glaciers or collecting geological specimens.

Over the years there have been variations of the Arctic Hut. A smaller version was made for a raft structure that is depicted in *Marooned on the Ice-Floe*. A visit to Nepal in 1991 allowed the same elements to become the Yeti Observatory, complete with binoculars and prayer flags; a larger installation, *The Last Yeti*, provided the Grand Hall with bamboo poles, gauze screens and flickering electric lights to recall the dim light of yak butter lamps. On that occasion the crackling radio was replaced by the sound of Tibetan monks chanting.

As an artist, I see my life devoted to making Naboland real. This involves a process of finding without looking, keeping an open mind to what might fit into this world. The application of traditional realistic drawing and painting skills, the abundance of visual stimuli in the form of book illustrations, the real and imagined travel imagery all seem to have created a mix that enables others to find for themselves something that sparks their own imaginative journeys.

In an earlier age my dream profession would have been to join explorers like James Cook or Charles Darwin as an expedition artist, and to document things unseen. My drawings and etchings try to evoke that sense of discovery; they often refer stylistically to illustrations of an earlier age, albeit in a more holistic approach which deliberately contrasts with the detailed documentation that modern research demands. The arrangement of objects in rows gives them a quasi scientific appearance that is often given a humorous twist due to their choice and juxtaposition. In my drawings, these ordinary things become precious through the time spent fashioning and engaging with them.

History

Edward Small

The Final Passage

I was twelve when I attended my first funeral. It was 1964, and, even now, memories of that day are clear to me. It perturbs me that I have no memory of what my great grandmother died of, and that her funeral looms larger in my mind than her death did, but then everyone dies, so death to me was less of a big event than attending that first funeral.

I picture a church, and the aged clergyman who conducted the event. He decided which hymns were sung, and he eulogised about this woman and made me realise how little I knew her. He told us she had been a tireless mill-worker, and made mention of how this loving wife was widowed in the First War. Apparently she was selfless and caring, and had a reputation as the perfect neighbour with boundless patience around children. I knew nothing of these things.

Nobody else talked at the church, and this continued as we followed the coffin and travelled in silent cars to the cemetery where he presided over the ceremony. Her coffin was a frightening box in shiny dark-brown wood, and it was lowered into the ground supported by cords that a handful of my male relatives held. He threw earth and a single rose onto it once it was lowered. 'Dust to dust', he uttered.

I remember feeling divorced from the proceedings. My mother and sister weren't there, but neither were there any other women present. I didn't cry at all; I didn't feel any urge to. I do remember consciously accepting that this particular funeral typified how we, in Scotland, had always disposed of someone, anyone, who had died. It would be

Edward Small
The Final Passage

almost fifty years later, and after much research in a subject that fascinates me, that I found out the gross inaccuracy of this assumption.

In August 1560, Scotland adopted Protestantism, with a haste and all-encompassing thoroughness that outdid any other country in Europe, and this despite having a Catholic queen. The ubiquitous Latin Mass was outlawed, and prayers for the souls of the dead, offered up that those departed might make their way to Heaven, were ended by John Knox's decree. The Scottish Parliament passed three Acts abolishing the Catholic faith, and reduced our Sacraments to two – baptism and communion. The funeral was no longer to be a religious service. Priests were given the option of becoming ministers, but all ministers were forbidden from conducting funerals. The logic was simple; *God makes his decision on your ultimate destination entirely based on how you lived your life, and prayers for the dead are both futile and an affront to our Creator. No amount of praying can undo His word, and therefore let all such things be set aside.*

In one fell swoop, the Church of Scotland abdicated authority over the disposal of bodies, though their General Assembly of 1563 ordered that '*uncoffined*' bodies should be buried in six feet of earth with no religious service.

And so it was. For the next three hundred and seventy years Protestant Scots buried their own dead and held their own, oft-times raucous, services. It wasn't until a decree from the General Assembly of the Church in 1929, entitled the Third Article Declaratory, that praying for the souls of the dead and ministering at funerals

was promoted and permitted. The funeral I had attended, that timeless, eternal, historical event as I thought it to be, was actually thirty years in existence.

This revelation was challenging. I had considered the funeral to be a constant; true, it was an entity with global variations but with the same unchanging routine and ritual within these disparate models. Death was *the* unique affair to me: we all die alone, we all die of unique causes and at different times in our lives. Many deaths may have been postponed by technological and medical interventions, meaning that death has become increasingly manageable, but it is never entirely predictable. My unshakable belief had been that the funeral and happenings around it were basically universal themes, and that death, like life, was immutably unique.

I was utterly wrong.

My first funeral, that one where women were absent, where the church dominated proceedings, where we stoically internalised grief in a shared experience, was not a timeless institution at all. Changes in the next fifty years would readily prove that. Whereas death, rather than being a unique inevitability, is, in any final analysis, the same for each and all irrespective of age, social standing, religiosity, health or mental condition, or even cause: it is, put simply, the cessation of life in every instance.

The funeral in Scotland now has as many females in attendance as males, and of all ages. Since 1968, and the beginning of women as ordained ministers, women have increasingly taken on the role as conductors of funerals: indeed they are disproportionately handling funerals in that the 25% of ministers who are women cover almost 50% of funerals. Records indicate that funerals most often retain a connection with religion - in 2015, 86% of Scottish funerals were conducted by people connected to the church - in a way that is not reflected in church attendance, but they also reveal a slowly growing drift towards non-religious events. The Humanist movement grew from the beginning of the 21st century, but even they, in their quasi-religious opposition to organised religion, are ceding to hitherto un-united civil celebrants with their apparently bespoke funeral handling. With these ever-growing possibilities and options, turning up at a funeral today can be a journey into uncertainty for mourners.

Grief has become an industry; since the arrival of Cruse Bereavement Care in the 1950s, who initially offered help only to widows, there is a raft of organisations handling different grief situations ranging from neo-natal to pets. All are worthwhile, all necessary, and all helping with a situation which used to be handled by communities and families. Grief is the mercurial factor around death; we all feel it, and humanity always has, yet we all experience different dimensions, and varying senses of loss, over individual deaths and about each death. Hymns have gradually ceded to popular songs, eulogies have become lighter and just as likely to celebrate the frailties of the deceased as any laudable traits. Chaplains, who often handle funerals where death has occurred in hospitals and hospices, are now in the employ of the NHS and have clock-in requirements and stringent rotas.

We now cremate two-thirds of our dead, and the post-1930 spurt in popularity of this option of disposal can be laid squarely at the feet of increasingly influential, and, dare I admit, increasingly affluent Funeral Directors, who have cultivated a tendency to dictate rather than be dictated to.

Coffins may be said to have changed, but there is an irony here. The 'uncoffined' bodies decreed in 1563 did not remain so for long. 'Uncoffined' bodies perforce have shape, show swellings, reveal weight loss or gain, all of which may allude to the causes of death. In the case of accidental death they may even describe too much. By the 17th century the coffin had returned, initially for the wealthier among us, but soon even pauper funerals had boxes. Coffins anonymise death, and the current, greater than ever, choice of styles may be a talking point, and may even reveal the proclivities of the deceased or the relatives, but they still serve, primarily, to deny us the presence of a body-shape. Coffins wrap the living in a cocoon of detachment just as much as they cocoon the deceased, and the effect is a desensitisation.

I do not know how my great grandmother died, but I know she died just as every other human being has, with the exception of we alive today. There is nothing unique in death: I repeat, regardless of circumstances it is the cessation of life. For those still alive, death is deprivative, regrettable, and always untimely. Those still alive are the mystificators, the conjecturers, the people who need to make sense or nonsense of death and its meaning. Like death, their ideas are as old as the hills, as old as time: as old as death.

Simon Jenner

Old Hall Manuscript, Supplement 1420:
Master Forest's Entry

Lord, accept my silvering gift of tongues
as I'm quartered by the moon's slow rasped breath
and light my way an inch farther down your service.
Here the isometric fuss has sloughed like dead skin.
My rhythms clean and shy in sixths, bite my youth –
never fresh itself, blackened in a gutter of small lamps.
The vigour shows in these new Glorias, imps
my scribe fetches with his exact raised eyebrows.
Let me gather in the Credos, Sanctus
for the ordinaries of the light-threaded winter:
if I must die, with a clutch of Agnus Dei
leaping over their tesssitura in the spring.

Poetry

Simon Jenner

Old Hall Manuscript:
Thomas Damett's Will

My will's legitimate, though I'm of a rive
a gent foisted with true heirs scratched from the earth.
Some yet recall time voided by death
when hours curdled over my Wiltshire with stilled bells
how our parents loosed screams from elders, caught
tagging in ruined hamlets where the black still lurked
till we scoured it all under. Sweet Mary, I've not shirked
your balm over what pestilence wrought.
Take my *Beata Dei genitrix* as our feet tread old hells,
let people and clergy, lady, draw out your breaths
on this fifth stall of St Paul's whilst I live
and dead may its singing draw my gentle birth.

Fiction

Jennifer Clement

The Scientist, Valentine and New York City

"She knows people believed eels were generated spontaneously out of mud and rotten meat created maggots. If they wanted to create a fly, honey was placed outside a window. If they wanted to create mice rags and corn were placed in a closet"

At Houston and Mott, on the sidewalk and beside a pile of large black plastic bags bursting with rubbish, there is an old, stained sofa and two wood chairs. There's a table lamp with a torn lampshade on the ground beside a transparent plastic sack filled with broken light bulbs.

Valentine thinks of the ghetto, eviction notices pasted on doors, windows smashed with stones, and furniture being thrown out into the street. She knows that evictions are in her heritage. She will pack her bags and need to get boxes from the supermarket. Will they divide up everything? Six plates for her husband and six plates for her? What about the silver? Who will get the painting? Her chairs will stand in a row out on the sidewalk and she will march with them away from her marriage.

Valentine moves away and leans against the window of the Milano bar. She looks inside. A rock poster pasted on the glass announces: Spontaneous Generation and Ice Pick play Saturday 10PM. Spontaneous Generation, Valentine hears the words inside. She knows people believed eels were generated spontaneously out of mud and rotten meat created maggots. If they wanted to create a fly, honey was placed outside a window. If they wanted to create mice rags and corn were placed in a closet. A rainbow was made from stones. A butterfly was made from dust and a piece of silk fabric.

Next to the Milano a small willow oak's branches are covered with used tea bags. The small Twinning Lapsang Souchong Tea red labels are intact and make the tree look as if it is covered with small red square leaves.

Valentine stands beneath the tea bag tree and closes her eyes. The bittersweet tea smell surrounds her. Within the aroma are Chinese boats and ports, the smell of rice and silk, the color red, and dragons. The smell of far away, of somewhere far from here.

Under the tea bag tree, she asks herself, Can you love someone you've never met? Can you love someone from the past, from another age? She knows the answer is yes and knows she is also of the dead people, that tribe, and the dustman's dust. Valentine loves a man. She loves a great scientist. She loves Louis Pasteur.

Under the tea bag tree she thinks. As a librarian, as a woman who is a keeper of books, time is found in words. Time is a verb tense. To love someone from the past is only a word tense. Listen: "This is the Past: When you came here, after spending the summer in Arbois, the experiments had waited for you. It was October. The accident of discovery was time. You knew that you could not make a moth from wood. You cannot make a woman out of breath. You were with me in the accident. I was waiting to tell you. I gave you everything you cannot see."

Do you hear? How Valentine changes time? Listen again: "This is the Present: When you are here, after spending the summer in Arbois, the experiments wait for you. It is October. The accident of discovery is time. You know that you cannot make a moth from wood. You cannot make a woman out of breath. You are with me in the accident. I wait to tell you. I give you everything you cannot see." You understand now? How time is only a tense in a book, a set of words? Listen one more time: "This is the Future: When you will be here, after spending the summer in Arbois, the experiments will wait for you. It is October. The accident of discovery will be time. You will know that you cannot make a moth from wood. You cannot make a woman out of breath. You will be with me in the accident. I will wait to tell you. I will give you everything you cannot see." "And there is Future in the Past" is what Valentine says "I had a feeling that I was going to know you and love you. That I was going to give you everything you cannot see."

Valentine knows all the books in the library on the scientist. There are the books on his discoveries of bacteriology, on disproving the doctrine of Spontaneous Generation, on crystals and on the rabies vaccine. In the present tense, she asks Louis Pasteur questions: "Did you hide the water in your house? When you have rabies you cannot even look at water, right? The thirst is terrible, right? You can drink so much you drown, right? Did you hide the water in your house?"

Valentine can hear him say, I always drank in secret. A windowpane can look like water. An empty glass holds the memory of water. I hide the glasses, pitchers, jugs and teapots and teacups. I pray it will not rain. Even light can look like water.

"What happened if it rained?"
I imagined the wolves in the forest.
"He was a rabid wolf, right?"

Jennifer Clement

The Scientist, Valentine and New York City

That's right, he says.

In one book about Louis Pasteur and his discovery of the rabies vaccine, there is a photograph of Joseph Meister taken in 1885. Meister stands with his elbow resting on a fringed armchair. Under the fresh, lanolin-smelling clothes there are fourteen dog bites on his hands, arms and legs. The cure was fourteen injections over a period of ten days. Joseph Meister was the first person to be inoculated.

Valentine read Pasteur's words: *Joseph Meister had been lifted up from beneath the dog covered with slaver and blood. At the examination of the dog it was proved that the animal was rabid as its stomach contained hay, straw, and scraps of wood. The death of this child appearing to be inevitable, I decided, not without lively and sore anxiety, as may well be believed, to try upon Joseph Meister, the method which I had found constantly successful with dogs.*

Valentine stands under the tea tree as two fire engines approach, the noise faint and stinging at first from afar, and then loud and high pitched as they race past. The sirens enter her ears and move throughout her body like an electrical shock. She looks up at the fire escape stairways that line the streets and looks for smoke.

Valentine thinks: When fate stood before you, doctor, you grew as tall as the doorframe and you closed your eyes. I kiss your eyes, here in the present, more than one hundred years away from you. Can you love someone you have never met? Can you love someone from the past, from another age? Yes and yes and yes.

Valentine moves to one side of the sidewalk, directly under the tea bag tree. The ground around the tree is dusted with loose tealeaves. Carved into the sidewalk is the date 1885. 1885, when the Statue of Liberty arrived in New York City aboard the French ship Isere and the Yiddish Theater opened, there were other children that Pasteur saved from rabies in New York City.

Under the tea bag tree Valentine can see them and they are only a few blocks away from where she stands: Four American children displayed in a store front at the Bowery in downtown New York. The youngest is five years old. They turn and bend like circus freaks. They show their arms and legs and lift up their shirts and expose their stomachs. On their skin one can see the red scars from the dog bites. Thousands of people come from all over to look at these boys and see for themselves if it is true. The boys' names are: Austin Fitzgerald, William Lane, Eddie Ryan and Patrick Reynolds. The same rabid dog bit all four of them. Under the teabag tree, Valentine hears microscopic sounds: eyes blinking around her, mouths opening and closing, skin against skin, words unspoken in the mind. There is the sound of an airplane overhead. The day is clear. The sky is a crystal, transparent glass framed by buildings, lampposts, fire escape ladders, awnings and trees. Valentine thinks, Before we could read, before there were even alphabets, we read the tracks of animals.

An airplane flies overhead. Far, far away. The day is clear. The sky is a crystal, transparent glass. She looks at the ladders of the fire escape stairways and thinks that they all lead to heaven. She thinks:

We read the ground, we read the animal tracks, and knew what walked there. We knew if there was a wolf in the forest. We knew if there was danger. The alphabet can be seen as animal tracks. Animals walk across the page. The letter Z is the track of a monster. It says I warned you. I warned you, husband.

The small square of sky between the buildings is filled with the white streaks left in the wake of airplanes. She asks: What can be known and what will always be unknown?

Louis Pasteur wrote, writes, will write: *Chance favours the prepared mind. Did you ever observe to whom the accidents happen? Chance favours only the prepared mind. Do not let yourself be tainted with a barren skepticism. It is surmounting difficulties that makes heroes. Let me tell you the secret that has led me to my goal. My strength lies solely in my tenacity. When I approach a child, he inspires in me two sentiments; tenderness for what he is, and respect for what he may become. Science knows no country, because knowledge belongs to humanity, and is the torch, which illuminates the world. Science is the highest personification of the nation because that nation will remain the first that carries the furthest the works of thought and intelligence. The universe is asymmetric and I am persuaded that life, as it is known to us, is a direct result of the asymmetry of the universe or of its indirect consequences. The universe is asymmetric. I am on the edge of mysteries and the veil is getting thinner and thinner.*

She can see him standing beside the window surrounded by vats, beakers, test tubes, funnels, small ovens and swan neck flasks. He is hiding water.

The New York sky is streaked with the long white ribbons of white jet fuel left in the blue atmosphere. Valentine breathes in the dust, plaster, glass, and shattered mirrors from the wreckage of the Twin Towers. The invisible, microscopic dust from the debris covers the city and will cover the city forever and ever.

I am on the edge of mysteries and the veil is getting thinner and thinner.

History

Annie Tindley

'Neither forgotten nor forgiven:'
the history of land futures in Scoland

"The power this family and
estate wielded was significant,
and on a national scale, so why
was their factor so worried?"

In the 1880s, the Highlands and Islands of Scotland were convulsed by a period of rural agitation
and revolt, known to contemporaries as the 'Crofters War', and by historians as the 'Highland Land
War'. This sometimes violent agitation was led by
the small tenants, or crofters, in the most remote
and rural parts of Scotland and ran roughly con-
currently with the 'Irish Land War'.[1] At its height
in 1886, the factor or estate manager for the
Sutherland estates wrote to his employer, the Duke
of Sutherland, with his advice for dealing with
the people, whose behaviour had – as he thought
– spiralled out of the estate's control since 1884:
'Let them understand that they must submit to
rule … The consequence [of conciliation] must be
that they will become more lawless and rebellious
against authority'.[2]

He was writing in the face of the most sustained
period of unrest and revolt seen for decades in
rural Scotland, and he feared the consequences of
a weakening of what he would have called *discipline* over the common people – the crofters, small
tenants and the landless cottars. But why was he so
concerned? The estates were enormous, the largest
in western Europe in this period, totaling around
1.2 million acres, including nearly all of the county of Sutherland plus holdings in Staffordshire,
Yorkshire and Shropshire. They were owned by the
earls and dukes of Sutherland, the Leveson-Gow-
ers, one of the richest patrician families in Britain,
who controlled a number of parliamentary seats
as well as a seat in the Lords and, in this period,
were Queen Victoria's favourites.[3] The power this
family and estate wielded was significant, and on a
national scale, so why was their factor so worried?

The Duke's fears stemmed from a growing recognition of the growth of different types of power and an awareness that traditionally effective methods of control – social, political and economic – were subsiding in the face of new, more assertive methods from the people that played out as disobedience, and perhaps most crushingly, in indifference. Control seemed to be slipping away from the hands of the estate management in Sutherland, the British landed classes, and aristocracy in general; a new definition of power, and of the balance between the rights and responsibilities of property, was evolving.

This story of the 'decline and fall' of the power and influence of Scotland's great landed families is a familiar one. From the 1880s, as the electoral franchise was steadily extended and death duties introduced, they faced serious and sustained legislative and social challenges to their financial, territorial and political powers.[4] And yet, in 2016, the Scottish Government passed a new Land Reform Act to tackle the concentrated patterns of landownership in the country. This Act is the last in a long line of land reform legislation passed for Scotland from 1886: why is such legislation still required? What will this reform hold for the land futures of Scotland?

Sutherland is a good place to raise such enquiries. Questions about the nature of power, land and space in highland Scotland are well framed here, a county dominated by one landed family until the 1920s. Sutherland is a prisoner to its history, particularly that of the clearances which affected all of the Highlands and Islands but Sutherland

most notoriously.[5] Arguably, the Sutherland family and estate have never been able to escape their historical reputation as great clearance landlords, no matter what estate management policies they introduced after the end of that period. Certainly, from the 1830s onwards, the family attempted in various ways to 'atone' for what had gone on in the past and we can see plenty of examples of relatively benign and forward-thinking policies through the nineteenth and twentieth centuries. Despite this, there has been no escape. Why? Because the *people* of Sutherland have also been unable to escape. Their ancestors were condemned to eke out a living on tiny, difficult plots of land, trapped by a structural poverty that thousands of people across three or four generations have lived in ever since.

But should land reform act as a historicist corrective, as a means of alleviating that sense of grievance that people hold, righting the wrongs of the past? Or should reform have primarily socio-economic aims for the country as a whole, redefining relationships of population to land mass? In order to think about these things we need to look at how people claim ownership and definition of land – from the crofter who claims it through occupation and work, to the landowner who claims it through title deeds, to other organisations such as conservation charities who claim to own or protect land for the benefit of society or the environment or for whatever their constituency is. Into this equation, the people who visit, enjoy, or work on aspects of land must also figure.

Annie Tindley

'Neither forgotten nor forgiven:'
the history of land futures in Scoland

Sutherland gives us a stark illustration of these questions. Very few places are as sparsely populated in European terms; an aesthetic of emptiness, created at the time of the clearances, is now engrained in popular culture as to what rural northwestern Scotland should look like. This has taken hold to the extent that some organisations seek to preserve this 'wild' land.[6] Yet what do we mean by this, and such aesthetic, Romantic traditions? How is a 'wilderness' still occupied and worked by committed communities? Should such wide, empty space be re-populated? Such representations and interpretations of the past and of history are the drivers behind much of the land reform debate today and associated debates around land use, space and power. And we need to sort through, disentangle such perceptions to be clear sighted in our understanding about Scottish land in general.

The first two themes relating to the perceived capabilities of the Highlands and what they should be 'for' arrive in the late eighteenth century. After the worst of the aftermath of the last Jacobite Rising of 1745 had passed, a growing sense of optimism flourished in and regarding the Highlands as a potential land of plenty, easily capable of economic development and prosperity, with some start-up investment and intellectual leadership to accelerate the process. New industries such as commercial fishing, kelp, black cattle and large-scale military recruitment, as well as the potential for new improved agriculture to transform the region into the breadbasket of Britain drove this wave of optimism. Such hope materialised as infrastructural developments – the building of General Wade's road, and later, Thomas Telford's efforts in road, canal,

bridge and church building (not necessarily in that order) – to connect the Highlands and far north physically to the southern markets; a population boom between the 1780s and 1860s; improvement projects and experiments all over the region.[7]

Alternatively, one can depict these changes as a clash between modernity and an agrarian, subsistence peasant society; modernity in the form of the birth of capitalism in Britain with landowners at its helm. The latter quickly recognised the opportunities of the industrial and imperial economy and some of them had the financial reserves to partake in this new world. Right at its heart was a re-definition of landscape and places in the Highlands, including Sutherland, cast as central to modernity and peripheral, as we might imagine today.[8] Rephrased as a question asked earlier, what do we want our landscape to be and what purpose should it serve? The answer given by Highland landlordism and the British state in the later eighteenth century was, as elsewhere – to be part of the new economy, the new society. To develop the opportunities of empire, of new wealth, to reinvent but keep some of the vestiges of the *ancient regime* – to keep the vestiges of deference and paternalism while reaping the rewards of capitalism.

From 1815, this optimism started to sour into negativity – a quality that has dogged perception, hardening into a certain kind of reality of the Highlands ever since. The economic crisis that came after the end of the Napoleonic Wars in 1815 crushed the Highlands and Islands; the bottom fell out of the market for kelp, the fish would not be caught, the growing population were thrown for their whole subsistence onto their small plots of poor land and the economy atrophied.[9] This is the beginning of the 'Highland Problem', as contemporaries were beginning to define it, and which is still with us today. The contours and definitions of this problem – seemingly intractable – have changed over the years, encompassing anything from overpopulation and congestion in the nineteenth century to depopulation and abandonment in the twentieth. But it has always had the clearances and the grinding poverty of the people at its heart.

In Sutherland we can even pin a date on the start of these processes: 1785, when capitalism came to the estate in the form of the Countess of Sutherland's marriage to Lord Stafford. The Countess brought vast but unprofitable acres in the north; Lord Stafford brought his industrial wealth and the Bridgewater inheritance. Together they applied them to Sutherland. With such a union, the Sutherlands embarked upon a process that would not end until the Land War of the 1880s, a process which attempted to make the Sutherland estates in the north economically self-sufficient and profitable. The first and most notorious result of this policy was what we now call the Sutherland clearances.

The clearances were carried out to accommodate a revolutionary change in the tenancy structure of the estate – a move from small farms to the consolidation of huge swathes of acres to accommodate large-scale commercial sheep farming. Some of these farms were enormous – Melness in the north of the estate stretched to over 80,000 acres.[10] The idea was that commercial sheep farming would drive the local economy and tie it to the national economy of the industrialising south and also to growing imperial markets; the bulk of the people, the small tenants, would now be crofters and given small plots of potato land on the coasts to support their chief new occupation, fishing. But the clearances were much more than an economic change, however revolutionary that might have been. They also led to a fundamental and traumatic adjustment in the lived experience and culture of tens of thousands of people.

This narrative returns us to the Highland Land War and the start of the legislative process for land reform that began in 1886. Land reform for the Highlands, and latterly for Scotland, has always rested on shaky grounds; right from the start it was explicitly constructed to right a historical wrong. As such, land reform has protected the crofting system and curbed the worst abuses of landed power, and positioned legislative reform as a deliberately backward looking process, undertaken to meet a need and an appetite to make good a historical wrong, in the form of the clearances and their long and short-term consequences. This appetite has overridden the competing need for reform to strike out towards the future, thinking widely and imaginatively about the nature of the relationship between power and land in Scotland. Instead, we are trapped by history as a comfort blanket: familiar positions taken up by familiar names and faces to rehearse the familiar arguments. Sutherland demonstrates a wider truth that everywhere in Scotland – from island to urban metropolis – is constantly a landscape in the making.

Sue Black

In Conversation with Edward Small

"My research is multidisciplinary, covering a wide variety of subjects including the detailed gross, micro-scopic and biomolecular analysis of adult and juvenile remains to establish all aspects of biological and personal identity including the sex, age at death, and disease and trauma status of the individual."

In the Queen's Birthday Honours List of Friday 11th June 2016, Professor Sue Black, Director of the Centre for Anatomy and Human Identification (CAHID) and Co-Director of the Leverhulme Research Centre for Forensic Science at the University of Dundee, was made a Dame Commander of the British Empire. She admits to being honoured to have received this award, but concedes that she is a little embarrassed too; emphasising a team effort, she observes, … it is certainly always encouraging for me and the forensics team here at Dundee to receive recognition because everything we do reflects on the team.'

How different things might have been if only she hadn't a fear and revulsion of rats, a phobia that she shares with broadcaster and naturalist, Sir David Attenborough. This fear made Sue decide to work on human bones during her fourth year at Aberdeen University, a project that grew into a love affair with the subject.

I wanted to principally ask her about body do-nation, and about the importance of the human cadaver to her branch of science. We went back immediately to 1981 when, as a young student she was being given her first cadaver to dissect. That incident came to her with great clarity: looking inside someone – the importance and the privilege of being granted this access – was and is funda-mental to her work:

My research is multidisciplinary, covering a wide variety of subjects including the detailed gross, microscopic and biomolecular analysis of adult and juvenile remains to establish all aspects of biological and personal identity including the sex, age at death, and disease and trauma status of the individual. We are working on some new and exciting multidisciplinary approaches to identification all underpinned by anatomical information and understanding.

Bodies donated to the University of Dundee are used for three specific purposes: firstly for anatomical examination, which concerns teaching of the structure and function of the human body to students and healthcare professionals; secondly for the education and training of healthcare professionals and especially for those undertaking surgical techniques; and thirdly for research, which involves scientific studies designed to improve our understanding of the human body in health and disease. Asked why models and simulated visual aids could not satisfy the same requirements, Sue is quick to point out that no two bodies are identical, and that she would much sooner be treated in a shoulder operation by some surgeon who had seen the vagaries and differences within a variety of bodies, than a doctor who studied only with a single model, irrespective of how life-like it may have been.

I asked whether there was an ample supply of donors, and to what extent any diminishing of the provision of bodies caused problems. She explained that when she was appointed Professor of Anatomy and Forensic Anthropology at Dundee in 2003, the University was making do with around thirty donated bodies per year. Universities, by law, are permitted to retain donated bodies for up to three years, and the low number of

donations meant that students were being asked to work with bodies that the previous year's students had already had the benefit of. 'Not ideal' was how Sue felt about the situation. Today the number of donations is nearer to three times the figure of ten years ago, and such increases can be put down to a few measures including the *In Memoriam Project*, the *Million for a Morgue* initiative and some positive publicity from relatives. Then, of course, there is Dundee's move to the Thiel embalming method.

Named after the man who developed it, Thiel embalming is a soft-fix method which leaves cadavers in a more realistic state, moveable and flexible. As well as markedly reducing the embalmers contact with Formalin used in traditional embalming methods, Thiel has opened up a whole set of research, training and educational possibilities which help to keep Dundee at the forefront of scientific advancement. The advantages drawn from the unique properties of Thiel-embalmed cadavers are pushing the boundaries of medical research and training. Sue explains that this comes at a financial price to the University, but her view is that 'one of the most selfless acts that a human can do is to donate his or her body to medical education and research, so we feel it is important, and respectful, to make the most of this wonderful gift. We have therefore invested heavily in our anatomy provision, building a brand new facility that brings a whole new perspective to body donation.'

She explains *Million for a Morgue*, and as she does so a smile crosses her lips. Apparently the public were asked to not only donate money to the campaign, but to vote for which one of a group

Sue Black

In Conversation with Edward Small

of writers they would like the morgue to be named after. 'The leading crime writers who lent their support were Lee Child, Jeffery Deaver, Jeff Lindsay, Stuart MacBride, Tess Gerritsen, Peter James, Kathy Reichs, Mark Billingham, Harlan Coben and Caro Ramsay; oh, and of course , Val McDermid who went on to win it so we now have the Val McDermid mortuary.' She answers a question about the involvement of crime writers by explaining that her expertise in anatomy and forensic anthropology is often called on by crime writers looking to build a sense of reality into stories. 'Val [McDermid] is a sweetie you know, but she's a terrible woman. She rings me on the pretext of just having a chat or a catch up, then she'll ask about the detail of some case or other, or she'll ask what I'm working on now. She knows that I'm on to her, and I know that she knows that, and often the call ends up in a giggling session.' In a profession which can lead into all too many serious and distasteful episodes the need for occasional laughter and levity is obvious.

I ask about anonymity when donating your body, and Sue's answer is unsurprising. No name is divulged, either to staff or students, and the cadavers and body parts are recognised by a numbered label only. She readily admits that most groups of students confer a first-name on the body they are tasked to work with – Jeannie, or Mary, or Tommy, or some other such-like name that is used with utter respect but helps forge a sense of familiarity from which comes gratefulness on the part of the medical students. Sue explained that the University holds an annual service for donors to which families are invited. Students too come

to pay their respects and it is easy to see the level of gratitude they hold for their 'silent tutors' in the dignified way that the students behave and present themselves.

Donors, whilst they are still alive and well, do come into contact with the University, most particularly through the offices of Bequeathal Secretary, Vivienne McGuire, who was awarded an MBE in 2015 for her services to bequeathal anatomy - the first ever national honour for this role. The Anatomy Act (1984) as amended by the Human Tissue (Scotland) Act 2006 is the legislation that details the legal requirements surrounding the donation of a body to medical science. Scotland, alone in UK terms, retains the services of HM Inspector of Anatomy; however, since the 2006 Act, donated bodies can no longer be accepted posthumously. It is mandatory that the donor completes and signs the relevant forms and this can mean a visit or, in some cases, visits to Vivienne. All potential donors are informed that at the time of death, the next of kin, or a nominated person, should contact the University Anatomy Department; in this way, the involvement of family is crucial to the gift of a body.

On the question whether Sue, herself, still has a chance to work with bodies as much as she would want to, there is a pregnant pause and a slight intake of breath; and she smiles. Her interest in the workings of the human body is as great as ever, and teaching students, as often as she can, allows her to retain reasonably regular contact.

Sue is Director of the Centre of Anatomy and Human Identification and that puts many other demands on her time. 'Within the field of forensic human identification we work with the police and other investigative agencies to assist with both national and international crimes where bringing the perpetrator to justice is at the forefront of our achievements.' In being recognised as experts in several areas, the department's staff are regularly called upon to present evidence in criminal courts in the UK and overseas. Sue takes pride in explaining that over 400 cases per year come to CAHID from police forces across the UK. Never one to rest on her laurels, she points out that the University has increased its research disciplines recently with the introduction of new staff; experts in fire investigation, drug analysis, fingerprint enhancement and detection of explosives augment what was already a very impressive research portfolio.

Asked about her voyage in life and work, Sue sees the happenstance around taking a job in a local butcher's business at the age of twelve as being the start of her journey. Being literally up to the elbows in 'blood, bone, muscle, flesh, offal and such things' made her comfortable with what many of us would find difficult. 'It seemed a very natural progression from a butcher's shop into an anatomy department dissecting room to a mortuary assisting the police'. Natural curiosity helps too, and a workaholic mentality that has never left her. Asked about her most significant influence she taps her shoulder and tells you about the little old grandmother, long-dead, who still watches over her, and who is not averse

to tutting at injudicious decisions even today. 'Difficult to stray from the right path with such a presence', Sue says.

Sue Black's successes are things she downplays. She has been made a fellow of the Royal Society of Edinburgh, the Royal Anthropological Institute, the Royal Society of Biology, the Royal College of Physicians, and is an Honorary Fellow of the Royal College of Physicians and Surgeons of Glasgow. She worked for the Foreign and Commonwealth Office of the UK, and the United Nations, and her work in human identification brought an OBE for work in the war theatre of Kosovo. All of this and more she owes to that first dissection of her first cadaver in 1981. It's short wonder that her utter respect and gratitude to those generous, selfless souls who have donated the ultimate gift, their body, to science is as strong today as it was at the outset of her fascinating voyage.

Poetry

Jim Stewart

Sea

The sea has reversed its name.
It will return; but for now,
withdraws to its dreaming pool,
and leaves things alone.

All night it heeds the moon's rhetoric,
the suasive darkness heavy
from above and from below.
Its heart is grave and has depth
and breadth to think of,

remembering a time
when, unpopulated,
it had only itself to consider,
and nothing broke the surface, or could sink.

Notes

Jim Stewart, 'Vessel'

Paul's 'Epistle to the Romans' (chs.8-9) is a source for his famous medi-tation on Christian and non-Christian destinies. The *proems* to Genesis chapter one and (eventually) to the Fourth Gospel would prove to be, in time, the frame for all such meditations, including influential reflections by Augustine and Calvin.

Christopher A. Whatley, 'Auld acquaintance: Robert Burns at home and away in the nineteenth century'

The photo on page 20 is the statue of Robert Burns by George Edwin Ewing, erected in Glasgow in 1877.
[1] See Gerard Carruthers, 'Introduction', in Gerard Carruthers (ed.), *The Edinburgh Companion to Robert Burns* (Edinburgh: Edinburgh University Press, 2009).
[2] See Frank Ferguson and Andrew R. Holmes (eds), *Revising Robert Burns and Ulster: Literature, Religion and Politics*, c.1770-1920 (Dublin: Four Courts Press, 2009).
[3] See Sharon Alker, Leith Davis and Holly Faith Nelson (eds), *Robert Burns and Transatlantic Culture* (London: Ashgate, 2012).
[4] Colin Kidd, 'Burns and Politics', in Carruthers, *Edinburgh Companion*, pp.61-73.
[5] See Christopher A. Whatley, *Immortal Memory: Burns and the Scottish People* (forthcoming, 2016).
[6] See Ferenc M. Szasz, *Abraham Lincoln and Robert Burns: Connected Lives and Legends* (Carbondale, IL: Southern Illinois University Press, 2008).
[7] Nigel Leask, '"Their Groves o' Sweet Myrtles": Robert Burns and the Scot-tish Colonial Experience', in Murray Pittock (ed.), *Robert Burns in Global Culture* (Lewisburg, PA: Bucknell University Press, 2011), pp.172-88.
[8] See the chapters by Murray Pittock, Robert Crawford, Frauke Reiteimeier and Alan Rawes in Pittock, *Robert Burns in Global Culture*.
[9] Quoted in Leask, '"The Groves o' Sweet Myrtles"', p.174.
[10] George Veitch, *Pilgrimage to the Shrine of Burns During the Festival with the Gathering of the Doon and other Poetical Pieces* (Edinburgh: McDowall, Greig & Walker, 1846), p.9.
[11] See Tanja Bueltmann, *Clubbing Together: Ethnicity, Civility and Formal Sociability in the Scottish Diaspora to 1930* (Liverpool: Liverpool University Press, 2014), p.86.
[12] Thomas M. Devine, *Independence or Union: Scotland's Past and Scotland's Present* (London: Allen Lane, 206), p.89.
[13] Robert Collyer, *Historical Sketch of a Burns Statue, the McPherson Legacy of the City of Albany* (Albany: Weed, Parsons, 1889), p.49.
[14] Michael E. Vance, 'Burns in the Park: A Tale of Three Monuments', in Alker, Davis and Nelson, *Robert Burns*, p.216.
[15] Collyer, *Historical Sketch*, p.14.
[16] *New York Times*, 3 October 1880.
[17] Edward Goodwillie, *The World's Memorials of Robert Burns* (Detriot, MI: Waverley Publishing Company, 1911), p.125.
[18] Bueltmann, *Clubbing Together*, p.216.
[19] Goodwillie, *World's Memorials*, p.119.

Kim Kremer, 'The Coin Testers'

[1] Ahad Ha'am, 'Two Masters' in *Selected Essays*, translated by Leon Simon (Philadelphia: The Jewish Publication Society of America, 1912), pp.91-2.
[2] John Jeremiah Sullivan (ed.), *The Best American Essays* (Boston and New York: Mariner Books and Houghton, Mifflin Harcourt, 2014), p.xxiv.
[3] Werner Herzog 'Minnesota Declaration' 1999, http://www.walkerart.org/magazine/1999/minnesota-declaration-truth-and-fact-in-docum (accessed 06 July 2016).
[4] J B Priestley, 'On Beginning I for One (1923)' in *All about Ourselves: And Other Essays* (London: William Heinemann, 1956), p.1.
[5] Phillip Lopate, *Portrait Inside My Head* (Widworthy Barton Honiton Devon: Notting Hill Editions, 2015), p. xiii.

Kim Adamson & Wendy Gammie, 'The story of RRS Discovery'

[1] Ann Savours, *The Voyages of the Discovery: An Illustrated History of Scott's Ship* (Barnsley: Seaforth, 2013) p.9.
[2] Tom Griffiths, *Slicing the Silence: Voyaging to Antarctica* (Cambridge: Harvard University Press, 2007), p.113.

Notes

Merran Gunn, 'Lullaby'

[1] Kirsty Gunn, *The Big Music* (London: Faber & Faber, 2012), p. 414.

Jeremy Ponyting, 'But England... What do you want with England?'

[1] The John Hearne quote comes from an essay, 'The Fugitive in the Forest:
Four Novels of Wilson Harris', *The Islands in Between* (Oxford: Oxford
University Press, 1969), p. 149.
[2] Kali Mai pujas are prayer meetings devoted to the female goddess Kali,
involving drumming, possession, sometimes animal sacrifice and acts of
healing. The rites came to Guyana (and to a lesser extent Trinidad) with
the small number of South Indian Madrassis who came as indentured
labourers between 1838-1917.
[3] Cumfa is an African Guyanese ceremony that begins in the tones
of Afro-Christianity but becomes progressively more African as the
night progresses. It involves dance, drumming, possession and healing.
Drummers are famed for their ability to exercise psychological control
over participants.
[4] Lyndon Forbes Burnham (1923-1985) was with Cheddi Jagan one
of the founding figures of Guyanese nationalism and anti-colonialism.
He split from Jagan in the 1950s and thereafter led a predominantly
African-Guyanese supported party. His Co-operative Socialism was widely
referred to as Corruperative and the collapse of the state-run economy sent
many thousands of Guyanese to North America. He came to power with
British and American help in 1966, and thereafter his PNC party rigged
elections until 1992.
[5] See S. D. Smith, *Slavery, Family and Gentry Capitalism in the British
Atlantic: The World of the Lascelles, 1648-1834* (Cambridge: Cambridge
University Press, 2006). The Lascelles' connection with sugar lasted until
the 1970s, when their last Barbadian estate was sold.
[6] The bitter irony, of course, was that whilst owners of slaves were
compensated for the surrender of their human property, the ex-enslaved
were never compensated for their forced labour, a matter at the heart of
the current demand for reparations. See Nicholas Draper, *The Price of
Emancipation: Slave-Ownership, Compensation and British Society at the
End of Slavery* (Cambridge: Cambridge University Press, 2009).

WN Herbert, 'The Dream of the Airport' was first published in *DURA*
(*Dundee University Review of the Arts*: www.dura-dundee.org.uk).

Amit Chaudhuri, 'Fredric Jameson's Strange Journey'

[1] Frederick Nietzsche, *The Birth of Tragedy*, https://archive.org/stream/
BirthOfTragedy/bitrad_djvu.txt
[2] Ranajit Guha, *History at the Limit of World-History* (New York: Columbia
University Press, 2002)
[3] Edward Said, 'Thoughts on Late Style', *London Review of Books* 26(15),
2004, pp. 3-7.
[4] Quoted in http://www.hindustantimes.com/india/nothing-but-a-poet/
story-KANphoqZR6whgnVOXJ1FwJ.html
[5] Fredric Jameson, *The Modernist Papers* (London: Verso, 2007).
[6] Fredric Jameson, *Postmodernism, Or, The Cultural Logic of Late Capitalism*
(Durham: Duke University Press, 1991).
[7] Fredric Jameson, *A Singular Modernity* (London: Verso, 2002), p.17.
[8] Harold Bloom, *A Map of Misreading*, Second edition, (Oxford: Oxford
University Press, 2003), p.36
[9] Richard Rorty, 'Against Belatedness', *London Review of Books*, 5(11),
1983, p. 3.
[10] Pierre Macherey, 'The Literary Thing', translated by Audrey Wasser,
Diacritics 37(4), 2007, pp.21-30.
[11] Peter D McDonald, 'Ideas of the Book and Histories of Literature: After
Theory', *PMLA Journal* 121(2006), pp.214-28.
[12] AK Ramanujan, 'Three Hundred Ramayanas: Five Examples and
Three Thoughts on Translation' in *The Collected Essays of A.K. Ramanujan*
(Oxford: Oxford University Press, 2004), p. 143.
[13] Fernando Pessoa, *The Selected Prose of Fernando Pessoa*, transl., ed.
Richard Zenith (New York: Grove Press, 2001).
[14] Pessoa, Fernando, *The Keeper of Sheep, transl.*, ed. Edwin Honig and
Susan M Brown (Riverdale-on-Hudson, New York: The Sheep Meadow
Press, 1985).

Jane Goldman, 'Discovery Woolf'

[1] Virginia Woolf, 'A Sketch of the Past', *Moments of Being*, ed. Jeanne Schulkind, 2nd Edition (London: Grafton, 1989).
[2] Woolf's ten novels are: *The Voyage Out* (1915), *Night and Day* (1919), *Jacob's Room* (1922), *Mrs. Dalloway* (1925), *To the Lighthouse* (1927), *Orlando: A Biography* (1928), *The Waves* (1931), *Flush: A Biography* (1933), *The Years* (1937), *Between the Acts* (1941).
[3] Virginia Woolf, *The Diary of Virginia Woolf* (5 vols.), ed. Anne Olivier Bell and Andrew McNeillie (London: Hogarth, 1977-1984).
[4] Jim Stewart, 'Classical shock in The Voyage Out', *The Voyage Out: Centenary Perspectives* (London: Virginia Woolf Society of Great Britain, 2015), p. 77.
[5] Virginia Woolf, *To the Lighthouse* (London: Hogarth, 1927).
[6] Virginia Woolf, *A Room of One's Own* (London: Hogarth, 1929).

Simon Jenner, 'Old Manuscript poems'

The Old Hall poems are from a sequence of about 25 poems on composers whose names, and sometimes details, are to be found in a manuscript from c.1410-1422 containing names of Medieval composers. Much of the music from the pre-Reformation period is lost but some of the more famous names such as John Dunstaple were for instance retrieved from book bindings in Croatia. It shows how far British music, with its *Contenance Angloise,* travelled.

This was the one time, until the Beatles, that British music was positioned at the cutting edge of European music. The French widely admired it, amidst the bloody and intermittently cultural interchanges of the Hundred Years' War (1340-1453), against which this music was written. It is contemporary for instance with The Agincourt Carol of 1415.
A parallel Scottish tradition was hugely encouraged by James I till his death in 1437, and the fifteenth Century *A Scottish Ladymass* reflects this. Most famous from the Scottish Renaissance was, of course, Robert Carver (c.1480-1568) who particularly flourished in the equally culturally alert court of James IV. There were important fifteenth century interchanges with English and Scottish composers.

Of the two presented here, Master Forest (his first name is unknown) was part of a supplementary group of composers in another hand, added after the original compilation, and reflecting a newer style of composition, away from what are now called isorhythms. Thomas Damett was the illegitimate son of a Wiltshire gentleman who resided in the Fifth Stall of the old St Paul's. We know this from a will dated 1437 that has survived. Damett is only slightly better documented than many others; some composers we know only by their surname and can only infer from their styles in surviving musical scores. I wrote the poem I in two stages, only realizing that Damett was the same person named in the will after I'd first drafted it. Several composers attended Henry V at Agincourt, and later. The death of Thomas First Duke of Clarence, younger brother of Henry V in 1421 seems to draw the compilation of the Old Hall manuscript to a close, with a lament on him: it most likely originated from his household.
In both instances, I've referred to pieces found in the Old Hall, now in the British Museum. Any puns and other perpetrations are mine.

Jennifer Clement, 'The Scientist, Valentine and New York City' is an excerpt is from her forthcoming novel, *Stormy People.*

Annie Tindley, '"Neither forgotten nor forgiven": The History of Land Futures in Scotland'

[1] See the classic account in J. Hunter, *The Making of the Crofting Community* (Edinburgh: John Donald, 1976); and A. Newby, *Ireland, Radicalism and the Scottish Highlands, c.1870-1912* (Edinburgh: Edinburgh University Press, 2007), pp. 1-8.
[2] National Library of Scotland, Sutherland Estates Papers, Acc. 10225, Policy Papers, 215, 22 Jan. 1886.
[3] A. Tindley, *The Sutherland Estate, 1850-1920: estate management, aristocratic decline and land reform* (Edinburgh: Edinburgh University Press, 2010), p. 1.
[4] D. Cannadine, *The Decline and Fall of the British Aristocracy* (London: Penguin, 1990); T. Dooley, *The Decline of the Big House in Ireland* (Dub-

lin: Wolfhound Press, 2001).
[5] E. Richards, *Debating the Highland Clearances* (Edinburgh: Edinburgh University Press, 2007), pp. 52, 55-6.
[6] See the project undertaken by Scottish Natural Heritage, *Mapping Scotland's Wilderness and Wild Land* (June 2014): http://www.snh.gov.uk/protecting-scotlands-nature/looking-after-landscapes/landscape-policy-and-guidance/wild-land/mapping/ (accessed 30 May 2016).
[7] Richards, *Debating the Highland Clearances,* pp. 49-53.
[8] F. Jonsson, *Enlightenment's Frontier: the Scottish Highlands and the origins of environmentalism* (Yale: Yale University Press, 2013).
[9] Richards, *Debating the Highland Clearances*, pp. 56-59.
[10] M. Bangor-Jones, 'Sheep farming in Sutherland in the eighteenth century, *Agricultural History Review,* 50 (2002), pp. 181-202.

Jim Stewart, 'Sea' was first published in *DURA* (*Dundee University Review of the Arts*: www.dura-dundee.org.uk)

All poetry readings can be found at:
https://dura-dundee.org.uk/category/the-voyage-out/

Contributors

Kim Adamson works as a sales and marketing officer at Dundee Heritage Trust.

Chris Arthur is author of five essay collections, and was a Royal Literary Fund Fellow at the University of Dundee from 2014-2016. Details of his writing, awards, and work in progress are available at www.chrisarthur.org.uk

Reinhard Behrens was trained in Fine Art at Hamburg College of Art. A German Academic Exchanged Service grant initiated his Scottish life at Edinburgh College of Art in 1979 and in 1995 he started an ongoing lectureship in drawing at Duncan of Jordanstone College of Art and Design.

Sue Black DBE, FRSE is Professor of Anatomy and Forensic Anthropology, and Director of the Leverhulme Research Centre for Forensic Science at the University of Dundee. She has assisted in war crimes investigations in Kosovo and with identification of the deceased in Sierra Leone, Iraq, Grenada and Syria.

Amit Chaudhuri is an award-winning author of six novels, the latest of which is *Odysseus Abroad*. In 2013, he was awarded the first Infosys Prize in the Humanities for outstanding contribution to literary studies. He is Professor of Contemporary Literature at the University of East Anglia and a Fellow of the Royal Society of Literature. He is also a critic, musician and composer.

Jennifer Clement is an award-winning novelist, poet and the President of PEN International. She is the author of *Prayers for the Stolen, A True Story Based on Lies, The Poison That Fascinates*, and *The Next Stranger*. She has also written a memoir, *Widow Basquiat*, on New York City in the early 1980's and the painter Jean-Michel Basquiat. More information is available at www.jennifer-clement.com.

Brian Cox is an actor, equally at home on stage, in films and in television. Amongst a plethora of honours, he has won the prestigious Olivier Award, and in 2002 was given a CBE. In 2010 he was appointed Rector at his home town University in Dundee. He puts a deep interest in social history down to his Irish and Scottish 'genes'.

Peter Davidson is Fellow of Campion Hall, University of Oxford. His most recent books have been *The Last of the Light* (Reaktion, 2015), a cultural history of twilight, and *Distance and Memory* (Carcanet, 2013), a book of essays on northern places.

Alison Donnell is Professor of Modern Literatures in English at the University of Reading, UK. She has published widely on Caribbean and black British writings, including a book-length revision of literary history,

Twentieth Century Caribbean Literature: Critical Moments in Anglophone Literary History (Routledge, 2006). She is co-editor, with Michael A. Bucknor, of *The Routledge Companion to Anglophone aribbean Literature* (Routledge, 2011).

Dundee International Women's Centre provides a wide range of social and learning opportunities, from driving theory and computing to conversational English and Arabic, supporting women to gain skills and confidence and to meet with other women from around the world.

Wendy Gammie works as events manager at Dundee Heritage Trust.

Jane Goldman is Reader in English at Glasgow University and a poet. She is a General Editor of the Cambridge University Press Edition of the Works of Virginias Woolf, and author of a number of books on Woolf, and on modernism and the avant-garde. *Border Thoughts* (Leamington Books, 2014) is her first volume of poems.

Gary Gowans is Course Director in Graphic Design at Duncan of Jordanstone College of Art & Design, Dundee. His practice in communication design encompasses traditional and contemporary media, and has involved many national and international partners including the MoD, Imperial War Museum, Alzheimers Society, NHS, and the Kyoto Institute of Technology.

Merran Gunn is a painter and ceramicist working in Caithness and has exhibited widely, there and in Edinburgh and London. She has worked with the University of Dundee before in a variety of projects connecting text and image, performance and music.

Ron Hay is Professor of Molecular Biology in the Centre for Gene Regulation and Expression at the University of Dundee and is a fellow of the Royal Society. His lab is focused on determining the molecular basis for drug action and has a particular interest in the use of arsenic in cancer therapy.

WN (Bill) Herbert is Professor of Poetry and Creative Writing at Newcastle University, and Dundee Makar. He was given a Cholmondeley award in 2014 and in 2015 became a Fellow of the Royal Society of Literature. He is mostly published by Bloodaxe Books; his most recent titles are *Omnesia* and *Omnesia Remixed*, and *Murder Bear*.

Simon Jenner has been the Director of Survivors' Poetry since 2003, and is RLF Grants and Fellow, UEL/Chichester. In 2014, he was Residency Poet in the City at Hackney Library. He is the author of *About Bloody Time* (2006), *Wrong Evenings* (2011), *Two for Joy* (2013), *Pessoa*

(Perdika). An Agenda Edition sequence of four books *Airs From Another Planet,* and *Propertius Elegies Book I* *(*Perdika*)* are both forthcoming. His poem, 'Peter Philips' Part Book Talks to Brueghel' was commended in the 2015 National Poetry Competition.

Kim Kremer worked in Children's Publishing for several years before joining Notting Hill Editions as Editorial Director in 2014. She lives in Cumbria.

Pat Law studied Drawing and Painting at Edinburgh College of Art and Ecological Sciences at Edinburgh University. Her work is prompted by observation of the landscape and cultures encountered through sailing voyages or travel, extending over a range of visual media and forms, often with materials closely linked to the environment. She runs Heriot Toun Studio, a multi-purpose award winning residential arts space in the Scottish Borders.

Robert Macfarlane is the author of a series of books about landscape, memory and imagination, including *Mountains of the Mind, The Wild Places, The Old Ways*, and most recently *Landmarks*. He is presently deep into a book about subterranea called *Underland*. He is a Fellow of Emmanuel College, Cambridge.

Lindsay Macgregor holds a PhD in History from the University of St. Andrews. She completed an MLitt in Writing Practice and Study at the University of Dundee in 2013 and received a New Writer's Award in 2015 from the Scottish Book Trust. Lindsay returns frequently to teach on the Creative Writing programme at Dundee and co-hosts Platform, a regular music and poetry night at Ladybank Station.

Beth McDonough studied Silversmithing at GSA, completing her MLitt in Writing Practice and Study at Dundee. Writer in Residence at the DCA 2014-16, her poetry appears in *Gutter, The Interpreter's House* and *Antiphon* and elsewhere; she also reviews and edits for DURA (Dundee University Review of the Arts www.dura-dundee.org.uk). *Handfast* (with Ruth Aylett), was published in 2016.

Vincent O'Sullivan is poet, short story writer, novelist, playwright, critic and editor. He was the New Zealand Poet Laureate (2013–2015) and was given the New Zealand Prime Minister's Award for Literary Achievement in 2006. His most recent poetry collection *Us, Them,* won the 2014 New Zealand Post Book Award for poetry; he has also co-edited the five-volume *Letters of Katherine Mansfield* published by Oxford University Press.

Jeremy Poynting took his first degree at the University of Leeds in 1968, taught for many years in further education and undertook a very part-time Ph D, awarded in 1985. He began Peepal Tree Press in the same year. He was awarded an honorary D.Litt by UWI Mona in 2015 and the Henry Swanzy Prize at the Bocas Litfest in 2016, both for services to Caribbean literature.

Manas Ray is a Professor in Cultural Studies at the Centre for Studies in Social Sciences, Calcutta. He is presently completing an anthology of his essays entitled, *Displaced: lives on the move*.

Jim Stewart took an MA in English at the University of Dundee in 1984 followed by a PhD at Edinburgh in 1990. A contemporary renaissance man, Jim was a scholar with research interests in Early Modern English Literature and Modernism, especially the work of Virginia Woolf and T S Eliot. He has been a regular reviewer for the *Times Literary Supplement,* and a Poet-in-Residence at Tentsmuir Forest (Fife). His poetry has appeared in *The Red Wheelbarrow, New Writing Scotland, Gutter, Northwords, InterLitQ* and elsewhere. He had also written a libretto for the opera Flora and the Prince.

Edward Small is a historian of death cultures, writer and playwright who teaches creative writing at the University of Dundee. He is the author of *Mary Lily Walker 1853-1913* and his acclaimed play, *Dundee's Four Marys,* consistently attracted sell-out audiences. His play *Pantomime of Death*, a play about funerals, premieres at the 2016 Edinburgh Fringe festival.

Annie Tindley is Senior Lecturer in history at the University of Dundee; her research focuses on modern rural Scottish history, with a particular examination of landed estates and aristocratic families. She is also the founder and Director of the Centre for Scotland's Land Futures, a collaborative, inter-disciplinary body investigating Scotland's land issues within a British and European context.

Christopher A Whatley OBE, FRSE is Professor of Scottish History at the University of Dundee. He is the author of the highly acclaimed *The Scots and the Union: Then and Now* (EUP, 2014). Publication of his most recent book, *Immortal Memory: Burns and the Scottish People* (John Donald) is imminent.

Acknowledgements

Kirsty Gunn and Gail Low would like to thank the School of Humanities at the University of Dundee and Dundee Heritage Trust for their support, and to David Graham for sound advice on publishing matters. Thanks also to Kuban Freeman for providing footprints at Tayport beach. We are grateful for help from Lindsay Macgregor and Edward Small, without whom this project would not have been completed.